EARTH

A Dowser's Investigation of Ley Lines

EARTH ENERGY

A Dowser's Investigation of LEY LINES

J. Havelock Fidler

THE AQUARIAN PRESS

First published as *Ley Lines* 1983
This second enlarged edition first published 1988

British Library Cataloguing in Publication Data

Fidler, J. Havelock
Earth energy : a dowser's investigation of
ley lines. — 2nd, enl. ed
1. Leys — Great Britain
1. Title   II. Ley lines
941   GN805

ISBN 0-85030-681-7

*The Aquarian Press is part of the
Thorsons Publishing Group, Wellingborough,
Northamptonshire, NN8 2RQ, England*

Printed in Great Britain by Woolnough Bookbinding Limited,
Irthlingborough, Northamptonshire.

3 5 7 9 10 8 6 4 2

Contents

Details of Figures

List of Plates

For
ETHEL
who really started it all,
and who has continued to encourage.

Author's Note

To those who read *Ley Lines,* the first edition of this book, and have any recall of what was said, I would suggest that they skip Chapter 1. This is simply a repeat of the original Chapters 1 and 2 and is here included as an introduction for new readers. The chapter on Ley Hunting has been greatly extended, correcting some of the original errors and sorting out previously unsolved problems. The many lines on the Shieldaig Peninsula are dealt with in fuller detail in Chapter 9.

The next three chapters have been largely rewritten, in order to remove the mathematics which apparently proved such a stumbling block to many readers. They were included so that any of my fellow scientists who should read this book might find that there was some truth in it, and that I was not basing my conclusions on a lot of wild and unsupported assumptions. That this was not entirely without success was proved by many of the letters I received. These mathematics are now banished to the various appendices, where they are available for anyone wishing to see this supporting evidence.

The effects of dowsable energy on plant growth, a subject which was barely touched on in the first edition, are now considered in much fuller detail in Chapter 6, while Chapters 7 and 8 deal with the many other properties of dowsable energy lines which I have investigated. The conclusions discussed in Chapter 10 have been completely reconsidered in the light of all I have discovered since writing *Ley Lines*.

For the Gaelic names of places, I have adhered strictly to the spelling on the Ordnance Survey maps, however erronous this may appear to be, so that readers may more readily find these places. The translations are based on the versions considered most correct by the various authorities I have consulted.

Acknowledgements

This second edition would never have been undertaken but for the many suggestions and questions (which I could not at the time answer) from the readers of the first edition. Too many to thank individually either wrote or called here with their many constructive comments.

Besides those mentioned in the first edition, the Burton family has again helped, this time in the person of Philip who has kept me in line with the many archaeological aspects of the subject. The Dowsers have also again helped, especially in the supply of the vital sample of Bluestone by Hugh and Libby from Prescelly. This, as the reader will appreciate, really gave the second edition its main theme and solved many of the outstanding problems.

My one-time colleague at Leeds, Jim Neald, also helped considerably by providing me with a supply of farm seeds with which to conduct my experiments in plant growth. Peter Huizinga, of Vageningen, also gave me much assistance over my difficulties in measuring surface tension etc. I am also indebted to our present mobile librarian Ian Fraser, who did his best to find for me some information on geo-magnetism, unfortunately without a great deal of success.

Finally, I must thank our nephew Robert Simpson for spending his week of annual leave in checking the typescript and offering many helpful suggestions, particularly over the vexed question of the Gaelic names and their translations, and I must add that I shall be eternally grateful to Bob Sephton for proving with his Cathode Ray Oscilloscope, beyond reasonable doubt, that it was not all just imagination.

Preface to the Second Edition

Having discovered that energy lines flowing between charged stones could be detected by dowsing, the research described in this book was undertaken in the hope that, by studying such lines, some light might be thrown on the mystery of ley lines. Since writing the first edition, however, there has been much discussion of this subject and, unfortunately, some confusion over what exactly is meant by the term ley line. A number of authors [25, 13] have attempted to sort out this problem, but I think the whole position is best illustrated by recounting a mythical story of the future:

'Once upon a time, round about the year AD 4000, a wise old man was sitting on his horse regarding the countryside in the area which used to be called Herefordshire (he was on a horse because, of course, all the fossil fuel deposits had been used up by then). He noticed that tall metal towers dotted about the countryside, with which he was quite familiar, appeared to be sited in straight lines, and he formed a theory that these towers marked the direction of the network of motor-ways which he believed existed in the late twentieth century. With great insight, he called these alignments "el-lines". The hunting of their remains became a popular sport and many clubs of el-hunters were formed.

'It soon became obvious that his theory that these towers were connected with motor tracks was not correct, but nobody could think of a good reason for their being in straight lines. The few archaeologists who took any interest in them, said they were not man-made because there was no broken crockery in the soil around them (they did not know that twentieth-century man only used plastic utensils, which had

long since degraded away.) Others said they marked the path
of ritual processions. Statisticians got out their calculating
machines and decided that there were so many of these
objects that it was possible to draw straight lines through any
number of them purely by chance.

'Finally, some dowsers came along with their weird
collection of instruments — pendulums, forked sticks, Oasis
Rods, etc. — and said that these towers had been used for
power transmission, and that they could, in fact, detect the
remnants of energy flow in these lines. The archaeologists said
that this was nonsense; every one knew that twentieth-century
man was just a painted barbarian who went about wearing
tight blue leggings (jeans?) and making horrible noises which
he called "pop-music": he could not possibly have known
anything about energy transmission. Anyway energy was not
transmitted along lines but through the air, even if this had
been discovered by Nichola Tesla early in the twentieth-
century, it was immediately forgotten and not discovered
again for several centuries. The el-hunters said who cared
anyway and went on with their el-line hunting, which was a
good thing because it got them out of their air-conditioned
hovels. Finally all the towers were pulled down because the
farmers wanted the material and they got in the way of the
flying saucers.'

This story is, of course, completely apocryphal, but it does,
I think, illustrate what happens when different groups become
interested in a phenomenon which is 'not clearly understood'
as scientists like to say. Unfortunately, each sect becomes
entrenched in its own particular theory and considers any
other as rank heresy, little short of blasphemy, to be extirpated
with the greatest rigour. This, of course, leads to a regular
field-day amongst 'the media' who take a delight in debunking
all and sundry.

I am afraid that in the first edition I was guilty of confusing
the overground energy lines, which were my main subject of
study, with the term 'ley line' which must be confined to the
type of alignment described by Watkins. In the present edition
I have tried to use the term 'energy line' for those lines which I
found flowing between my charged stones. The dowsers [25]
suggest the term 'dowsable energy line', but I have tended to
drop the 'dowsable' because it is obvious that the lines

detected were mostly by dowsing. Even so, it became clear during the progress of this work that all real ley lines are, in fact, energy lines, but, of course, not all energy lines are ley lines. For example, Black Lines and geodetic lines are dowsable but are certainly not true ley lines. Sig Lonegren, in a recent article [30] goes so far as to maintain that if an alignment does *not* have dowsable energy flowing along it, one must consider it to be only a 'pseudo-ley', i.e. a chance alignment of ancient monuments.

The work described in this book was undertaken as a scientific study of these energy lines, with the hope that a knowledge of their properties might lead to some solution of the problem of ley lines and why they were set up. In doing this I have used a number of dowsing techniques in my experiments. Dowsing is a very suspect subject amongst many scientists and I feel I should say something to justify its use in scientific research.

This art of dowsing is another subject which is not clearly understood, and many sceptics go so far as to say that it does not really exist at all; but sceptics are, of course, notorious for being ignorant of the relevant literature. [31] They tend to point out that dowsers claim to detect forces which are barely or not at all recorded by the most sensitive of modern instruments; that the human body could be so sensitive, they say, is clearly absurd, so the dowsers' claim must be false. In the course of describing my work in this book, I shall show that with a pendulum I was able not only to detect, but also to measure, with a reasonable degree of accuracy, the residual magentism in igneous rocks, and also the daily fluctuations in the terrestrial magnetic field, both of which were barely recorded on my magnetometer.

That the recording of a dowsing reaction is not sufficien; proof of the presence of a phenomenon in reality was pointed out to me in my very early days as a dowser by Major-General Scott Elliot, at that time the President of the British Society of Dowsers. He stipulated, very rightly, that any dowsing observation must be confirmable by other objective means. In the course of this work, I have developed, and will describe in some detail, entirely objective methods of measuring effects, discovered in the first place by dowsing, by means of bioassays, mainly with mustard seedlings. Wherever there was any question of the validity of my dowsing observations, these have been put to the test with such biological methods.

Where, then, does dowsing play a useful part in scientific research? Again it really depends on what one means by dowsing, and this is a very controversial subject. I think that the best definition is that it is a form of controlled intuition. It is now acknowledged by most philosophers of science that intuition plays a major part in scientific discovery and that it is an aspect of the right lobe of the human brain, as opposed to the more logical and articulate left side. Frequently on considering research data presented by my dowsing, I have been quite lost for a logical explanation; then on going to bed, my left brain had become unconscious and freed the right side to consider the data presented. In the morning a complete solution is present, which seems so simple that one wonders what all the difficulty was about.

Dowsing is a phenomenon of the right side of the brain and it resents any interference by the logical left brain. Hence it is best when dowsing to keep the conscious left brain as free as possible of any anticipation of the results, allowing the right side to indicate its conclusion by symbolic signals, such as the rotation of the pendulum or turning of the angle roads. This is where many dowsers confuse their results: either they ask a wrong or confusing question of their unconscious mind, and in consequence get a confusing answer; or they may not really have understood what was required of them. This is the cause of the failure of so many of the so-called tests carried out, particularly by the media, to validate the art of dowsing. For example, a number of dowsers are asked if they can find some object in a certain area. That they usually do so is to their credit, but their findings often differ from each other because they have not been clear as to what is required of them. Another confusion is that it is quite possible for one dowser to pick up another dowser's idea and for them both to create a 'thought-form' which is then picked up by both of them and, indeed, others. At the end of the first edition of my book, I gave an example of how two people can produce such a thought-form, in this case an energy line which was quite capable of charging a stone, such as is used so often in the present study. I have tried to guard against this artefact, as will be explained later in this edition.

Unfortunately, many dowsers are inclined to produce elaborate theories based only on their dowsing observations, forgetting that these observations are only their personal reactions to external reality and not reality itself. In this book I have tried to restrict the tendency to form hypotheses until the final chapter where I do put forward a few tentative conclusions. However, as that master of philosophy of science Sir Karl Popper has pointed out, [37] for an hypothesis to have any useful content of information, it must be potentially falsifiable. Thus it is never possible to prove conclusively that a theory is correct, however much empirical data is collected, but let one instance prove false and the whole edifice collapses.

In the present investigation I determined to collect as much data as possible on the nature of ley lines — something in the form of a Natural History of ley lines — and disregard all the various, generally unfalsifiable, theories which have been put forward in the past. This was mistakenly interpreted by some readers of the first edition to be an indication that I had not, in fact, read these works, especially if they were not included in my list of references. The latter is, of course, only a list of works from which I have quoted observations and certainly not a full bibliography of all writings on the subject of ley lines, which would alone form a work almost the size of the present volume.

I have little doubt that any geophysicist who might happen to read this book would consider that it is full of mistakes and false conclusions. I would hope, however, that he would not find any of the observations I have made of these phenomena incorrect. That I may have drawn some erroneous conclusions is certainly due to the fact that I am not a specialist in the subject.

A century or so ago it was just possible for a scientist to have a working knowledge of all branches of science (what was called a polymath) and when I was trained as a scientist some fifty years ago, this was still the object of my instruction. Such a feat is now beyond the powers of any one man, so vast has the range of knowledge become, and in consequence every scientist has become more and more of a specialist in his chosen subject, having little or no knowledge of other disciplines. Unfortunately, some specialists tend to resent the interest of amateurs in their subject, feeling that this only leads to the production of 'pseudo-science'.

This specialization has, of course, been of considerable loss to science as a whole, since many fundamental discoveries are made by finding that one can apply new knowledge of another branch to solve a problem in one's own discipline. This is only possible now by workers in various branches forming a team to solve a common problem. An important example of this is the great advances made by the 'New Archaeology', by applying the discoveries of carbon isotopes and Bristle Cone Dendrology, which has led to a complete revision of a prehistoric dating.

I trust, therefore, that any reader with a specialist's knowledge of geophysics will not look for my mistakes, but realize that my observations show that here is a problem which merits wider investigation.

1
Sling Stones, Cones and Lines

Just as I was getting out of the mobile library, Ethel handed me a book saying, 'Have you read this?' It was a book on dowsing by T.C. Lethbridge. Actually, I had been introduced to the art of dowsing some twenty years earlier, when I was living in Cardiff, but this had been confined to the use of the 'short' pendulum, i.e. a bob of almost any material on a cord about 8 inches (20 cm) long. The friends who introduced me to this art were mainly interested in medical diagnosis (radiesthesia) but they pointed out that dowsing could be used for many other purposes. As a totally inexperienced dowser, I felt that it was inadvisable for me to dabble with my own or other people's health, but I did try wielding the pendulum over various objects, and soon found that I could in fact dowse. In my hands, however, the pendulum insisted on gyrating in an anti-clockwise direction for the answer 'yes' to my various questions, and oscillate for 'no'. Sometimes the pendulum would gyrate clockwise, but the reason for this I was not to discover until much later, when I had read many of Lethbridge's books.[27] Soon after this first foray I abandoned dowsing until some twelve or so years later, when I discovered Lethbridge's books and I quickly found the subject quite fascinating.

I had recently retired from a long career in agricultural research and was looking round for a suitable subject to occupy my mind in retirement. My wife and I had bought a 100-year-old Presbyterian manse and its abandoned church in the small village of Shieldaig on the north-west coast of Scotland. This church building was to form an essential ingredient in my various researches into dowsing. Lethbridge had also been a retired scientist, and I found that his enquiring mind had investigated many intriguing aspects of dowsing and raised a host of unanswered questions. Here, then, was a fascinating field which I thought I could investigate. Adopting Lethbridge's methods, I soon found that I was a sensitive dowser, but one with much to learn about the art.

Lethbridge's methods were different from most other dowsers in that he used what is known as the 'long pendulum'. In this the bob is attached to a cord about 40 inches (1m) long. He found that each material over which the bob is held will 'cause' the pendulum to gyrate only if the length of the cord between the hand and the bob is of a specific length, and this he called the 'rate' for the material in question. He went even further than this, maintaining that there are specific rates for male and female and for such abstract concepts as truth, good, evil, death, etc.

It was not long before I had read all Lethbridge's books on dowsing and tried out his concept of rates. I found that these worked perfectly in my hands, except that the pendulum still went 'widdershins' when I had found the right rate for the material under examination. I found that the correct rate could be found by lengthening or shortening the pendulum cord; when it was too short the pendulum oscillated in a vertical direction, i.e. away and towards me; when it was too long, it oscillated at right-angles to this. When the correct length had been reached, these two motions combined to make the pendulum gyrate. Later, I discovered that, if the cord was twice as long as the correct rate, the pendulum would gyrate clockwise, and this was also true for a cord half the correct length. These are, of course, harmonic ratios, but whether this is of any significance or not I am not at all sure.

It is generally accepted that all of the 'tools' used by a dowser are no more than magnifiers of his small muscular reactions to signals from his subconscious. Whether these 'harmonic' reactions are simply a reflection of a somewhat mathematical subconscious mind, I am not too certain, but I did find later that there is some physical support for them. However, I found that these reactions worked well with me and enabled me to find many more rates than those published by Lethbridge.

One point that I should make clear before going further is that I am in the habit of measuring my rates, i.e. the length of the cord, in centimetres. The idea of this was greatly disapproved of by Lethbridge and he spent several pages in one of his books saying just what he thought of the metric system in general. His main point was that the range of rates was between 0 and 40 inches, and that, if these are marked out round a circle divided into 40 segments, contrasting concepts occur at opposite sides of the circle: e.g. life at 20 and death at 40. He maintained that this relationship would not work if a centimetre scale were used. As a scientist I have always used the metric scale and found it very convenient for measuring the length of the pendulum cord. Forty inches, as used by Lethbridge, is virtually the same as 100 centimetres (39.3708 inches), so there is little over half an inch difference in the longest rate, particularly as I measure my cord to the centre of gravity of the bob. Moreover, the ratio of opposite concepts works just as well: e.g. life is at 50 and death at 100 cm.

The harmonic ratios, I often find, are very useful in the field. A long cord of, say, 100 cm is very difficult to control in a wind, unless one has a very heavy bob at the end of it. I usually use a bob weighing about 50g (2 oz), and this does get blown about, so that it is difficult to interpret its movements. If, however, the cord is shortened to half, a positive reaction is given if it gyrates in a clockwise direction. One can even go down to a quarter-length cord, when the gyration will again be anti-clockwise.

In one of his books, Lethbridge describes how he and his wife found what he thought must be sling stones outside a hill fort some distance from the sea. These were rounded pebbles, obviously taken from the sea beaches, and he considered that they must have been brought up to the fort by men to use in its defence. He tested these stones with his pendulum and found they gave a reaction to the male rate (60 cm) and in addition a reaction to that for anger. Smaller stones only gave the male reaction, and he suggested that these had been used by boys practising their sling throwing. He and his wife confirmed this 'charging' of stones by each throwing at a wall stones collected (and previously untouched) from the sea shore. In each case a male or female reaction was given by the stone when tested with the pendulum. My wife and I repeated Lethbridge's experiment of throwing previously untouched stones collected from the sea shore and found that they gave the appropriate reaction with the pendulum. In addition, I happened to have a flint arrowhead, collected when I was living in South Wales. I tested this with my pendulum, using a cord 60 cm long, and found a strong male reaction. This meant that the original imprint may have persisted in this flint for some three or four thousand years.

About this time I had become interested in certain heaps of stones, which I had noticed scattered round some parts of the countryside near to Shieldaig. These heaps of stones appeared to be of two different kinds, the first of which was at the sides of cultivated ground, the stones being of all sizes, as were the heaps that they made up. These stones had obviously been mixed with the fine soil when the ice retreated at the end of the last Ice Age, picked out by the crofters as they laboriously cultivated the ground, and piled at the side of the field.

The other heaps were rather different from these piles of clearance stones. The stones were more or less uniform in size, usually about 2 to 4 inches (5-10 cm) across, and the heaps about 8 feet (2.4 m) long and about 3 to 4 feet wide (0.9-1.2 m) wide; very noticeably the long dimension ran approximately east and west. Testing these heaps with my pendulum gave a reaction for death (rate of 100 cm). I came to the conclusion, therefore, that heaps of this type had been used for burials, in the absence of any recognizable and easily available burial ground in the immediate district, Applecross being some sixteen miles away over the hills.

To explain this means going into the intricacies of local history. The area round Applecross was greatly influenced by the foundation of an abbey by St Maelrubha, one of the early Irish saints. This foundation persisted until the Reformation and the death of the last abbot in 1567. After this date there appears to have been no ecclesiastical representation in the Shieldaig area until the government built a Telford church and manse in the village in 1823 (not the one that I now live in). During the intervening period, Christianity appears, as far as one can judge, to have been rather in abeyance, and some of the old pagan beliefs were revived, in addition to an increase in witchcraft, which was never very far below the surface in the Western Highlands. Burial in consecrated ground would not therefore have been considered important or necessary.

I had also become interested in the technique of dating with the pendulum and had worked out a method for such estimations based on the binary system. [14] On applying this technique to some sixty or so of these graves, I obtained dates falling between 1600 and 1800. At the same time my pendulum had also indicated a male rate on all of these dated graves, as well as a female rate on about half of them; in no case did I find a female rate alone. I came to the conclusion that this imprint of both male and female on about half the heaps of stones was possibly due to the Highland custom of only men burying the women, whereas there was no case of female-only stone heaps, i.e. of women burying women. Here, then, was a good example of stones having absorbed a sex imprint of both the body buried in the grave and also of the men who carried out the burial. I was later to confirm this supposition by testing the stones on modern graves, where the sex of the internant was identifiable from the gravestone. The stones on these graves I had been examining were apparently imprinted in the same way as the sex of the thrower of Lethbridge's sling stones, and I decided therefore to investigate the imprint in more detail.

I soon found that it was not necessary to throw the stone at a wall to imprint it. If the stone was held in the hand and hit smartly with a hammer, a good imprint was obtained. If, however, a previously unhandled stone was placed on the ground and hit, even with a seven-pound sledgehammer, no imprint was obtained. This observation soon led me to discover that one could imprint an untouched stone by hammering it on the ground alongside another stone which had been previously imprinted by my wife with the female rate; the uncharged stone received the female imprint even though it was I who had done the hammering. On the other hand, if I handled the stone first, placed it alongside a female-imprinted stone and then hammered it, the stone would take on both a male *and* a female imprint, the pendulum gyrating with the cord lengths of both 60 and 72.5 cm. This produced stones with a similar imprint to those I had found on graves where a woman had presumably been buried.

Lethbridge found that all living material has an inherent male or female rate, and that this is retained even after death. As an agricultural scientist I was well aware that all soil is made up of ground-down rocks, together with the decayed remains (humus) of plant material and the micro-organisms that live in the soil. If all these maintained in their dead bodies their inherent sex rate, all soil would become charged with both male and remale rates. That this is not the case can readily be discovered by holding a pendulum of the correct length over some soil. What therefore happens to the dead material in the soil? As everyone knows it gradually breaks down into simple chemicals to form humus. In doing so, does this material lose its inherent sex rate? To test this I first examined a sample of freshly-cut grass mowings and found that this gave a strong reaction with the pendulum at both the male and female rates. This is hardly surprising considering the number of weeds in my lawn. I then examined a well rotted sample from the base of our compost heap, which is made largely from just such lawn mowings. There was only the faintest reaction to either of the sex rates, and a sod from our peat stack gave no reaction at all, as also was the case with a lump of coal. This seemed to indicate that as the dead material breaks down into simpler chemicals, the sex reaction is gradually lost.

This conclusion is well illustrated by a simple experiment. Take an ordinary wooden match and test its sex rate with the pendulum. In the one I used, the wood (spruce?) gave a female reaction. Now strike the match and allow it to burn out completely. This can be done by holding it in a pair of pliers and changing ends when the match is half burnt. Do not place the match on anything (for example a plate) while it is burning because, as I shall show later it would then become fixed with the charge of the plate. When cold, test the stick of the match for sex reaction. It now consists of almost pure carbon, perhaps with a few other trace elements, and it will be found that there is now no sign of the original sex reaction.

As my wife pointed out, this would seem to dispose of my theory devised to account for the sex reaction found in stones from what I thought must have been graves, as described above. I do not, however, think this is so. The bones of interred bodies usually last a considerable time and in a peaty soil, such as is almost universal in our locality, whole bodies have been found, complete with clothing, after thousands of years of burial. The graves I have described can all be classed as archaeologically very recent and it would seem almost certain that some remains of the body would still be present in sufficient quantity to give a sex reaction. This could, of course, only be proved by a detailed excavation of the site, which I am not qualified to undertake.

In many of his books Lethbridge pointed out that there is a circular field round an object, the radius of which is equal to the rate. Anywhere inside this circle the pendulum will gyrate if the cord is of the appropriate length, while outside this circle no reaction is obtained and the pendulum merely oscillates. I discovered that if a stone is hammered just outside this circle, no imprint is obtained, whereas the stone can be placed anywhere within the circle and it takes on the imprint of the 'parent' stone. It was this problem of these circular fields and their inter-relationships that I had to investigate next.

Cones and Lines

Another book to which Ethel introduced me was one by the late Guy Underwood.[48] This dowser had spent many years investigating the geodetic lines he found below such pre-historic sites as stone circles, including Stonehenge, barrows, dolmen, menhirs, etc., as well as pre-Reformation churches. He noticed three types of geodetic line: water lines , track lines, and what he called aquastats. The first of these he considered were the normal underground streams encoun-tered by water diviners, while the second were tracks which were often followed by animals and which sometimes

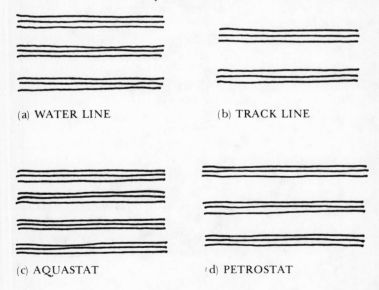

(a) WATER LINE   (b) TRACK LINE

(c) AQUASTAT   (d) PETROSTAT

Figure 1. Construction of geodetic lines.

developed into those frequented by man. Aquastats, in spite of their name, do not appear to be connected with underground water, and it is not clear why Underwood chose this name for them.

Each geodetic line is made up of a number of 'parallels', and each of these is triple in form, being called a triad by Underwood. Water lines are made up of three lines, each one being a triad (Figure 1), while track lines have only two such parallel lines of triads. Aquastats have four lines, each again being a triad. Underwood was at pains to point out that these geodetic lines, although travelling in a specific direction, do not proceed directly but wind and zig-zag, often in a very complex way. Water lines, he considered, were 'positive' and mainly affected the left hand of the dowser, whereas track lines and aquastats were negative and affected the right hand.

Underwood went on to describe many different forms of convolution in the main courses of his geodetic lines. Amongst these the most important is what he called a 'Blind Spring', this being a centre on which his primary lines converged. It was, he thought, in the form of a spiral with numerous coils. He went on to state that the blind spring was an esoteric centre of the Old Religion, forming the most important part of an ancient monument, this becoming 'holy ground'.

Underwood also described a number of instruments which he used in his work and which he found to be much more sensitive than the normal hazel or willow twigs used by water diviners. Amongst these he described the 'Oasis Rod', which I found so interesting that I soon made myself one (Figure 2).

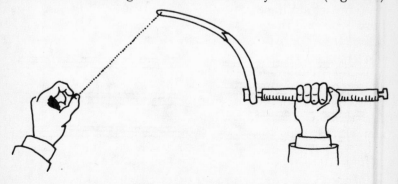

Figure 2. Underwood's Oasis Rod.

Full details of its construction are given in my article in the
Journal of the British Society of Dowsers. [15] Briefly, it consists of a
springy strip of brass attached at one end to an axle that can
freely rotate within a wooden handle, this being held in one
hand in a horizontal position. To the other end of the brass
spring is attached a light cord about 8 inches (20cm) long, the
other end of which is held between finger and thumb of the
other hand. In use, the held end of the cord must be exactly in
line with the axle, with enough tension to keep the spring in
the form of a quarter circle. If the cord hand is not in line, the
spring will flap about quite uncontrollably. The art, which is
learnt after a little practice, is to keep the spring in a horizontal
position, when minute alterations in the muscle tension of the
arm will cause it to rise or fall. It would appear from Underwood's illustrations that he kept the spring pointing inwards
towards the body, whereas I prefer to have it pointing out-
wards. After some years of use with this instrument, I have
found it extremely sensitive. As soon as one reaches a line, it
flips down and one can readily pick up the three lines of a triad
which are only a few inches apart.

Underwood's main thesis was that the layout of all ancient
sites were designed to coincide with the underlying geodetic
lines. As mentioned above, part of my Highland property is a
disused church building. Having mastered the use of the
Oasis Rod, I thought it would be interesting to see what, if any,
geodetic lines I could find in it. As the church was built only
about a hundred years ago, when presumably the masons and
architects were no longer familiar with the ancient lore, this
church would probably not knowingly be placed on what the
ancients would have considered to be a suitable site. It need
hardly be said that I found no sign of geodetic lines as described by Underwood, but what I did find was to set me off on
the main course of my future researches.

Before detailing these discoveries, it would be appropriate
to describe this church building since it was to form such an
important part of my work. It consists of a massive — the walls
are over three feet thick — rectangular building about 75 x 40
feet with the long axis roughly north-west to south-east. There
is a small vestry on the north-west end (Figure 3). It is constructed of rectangular, dressed Torridonian sandstone blocks
as facings, with rough stones mortared together on the inside.
Torridonian sandstone is one of the oldest rocks in the British

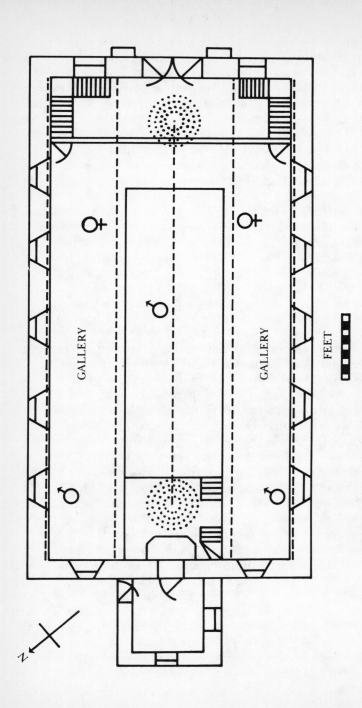

Figure 3. Plan of Shieldaig Old Church, showing energy lines and blind springs.

Isles and forms most of the mountains in the area. It is extremely hard. The other local rock is Lewisian Gneiss, which forms the bedrock on which the church lies. This latter rock is even more ancient, being formed in the Pre-Cambrian era, and is greatly contorted, thus being unsuitable for building purposes.

Inside the front door of the church there is a vestibule with stairs leading up on either side to a tiered gallery some 9½ feet from floor level. This gallery runs round three sides of the building and is supported on cast-iron pillars. There was originally a partition wall cutting off the vestibule from the main church area, with a door on either side, but this was removed at some date after the building ceased to be used as a church, to allow access for cars, the building now being used as a garage. At the north-west end is a raised area which was probably reserved for the Elders of the Church, and in the centre of this is a smaller raised platform with immediate access to the vestry door.

To return to my discoveries with the Oasis Rod, I found that there was a line down the centre of the building that reacted to the male rate of the pendulum and that there were two similar lines down the side walls. Immediately below the edge of the gallery and running between the iron pillars was a line which gave a female rate reaction with the pendulum. Furthermore, at each end of the central line was a complex which resembled the blind spring as outlined by Underwood. One of these had its centre in the middle of the vestibule and the other was just on the edge of the raised platform outside the vestry. Each of the above lines was a triad with side lines (parallels) at a distance of a foot or more on either side of the central line. I could find no sign of any lines in the vestry.

The question immediately arose as to the nature of these lines. Were they geodetic lines running through the underlying rock, or did they run somewhere through the air within the building? They certainly did not fit the main characteristics of the three types of geodetic line as described by Underwood. In that there was a central triad with parallel triads on either side at a distance of about a foot, these lines to some extent resembled Underwood's water lines, but I could not detect any sign of underground water even under the blind springs. Also they seemed to be far too straight for water lines. If these lines were not geodetic in nature, were they some form of aerial line?

After much thought on this problem, I recalled a diagram reproduced in several of Lethbridge's books. He had discovered that the circular field which surrounds an object such as a charged stone, is really the base of a cone that extends vertically upwards above the object. There is also another similar, but inverted, cone extending below the object. The radius of the base of the cone is usually equal to the rate of the charge, i.e. it is 60 cm for a male imprinted stone and 72.5 cm for a female (Figure 4a). Lethbridge did not, as far as I am aware, estimate the height of these cones, but, by placing a charged stone on the floor of the church below the gallery, I was able to measure the radius of the cone above and to calculate by means of a little simple trigonometry that the tip of the cone surrounding the male stone was about 13½ metres above the floor. By placing the stone on the gallery and measuring the radius of the cone below it, I was able to confirm that the lower cone was of a similar size to that above. I also repeated this exercise with a female-imprinted stone and was surprised to find that the tip of the cone was approxi-

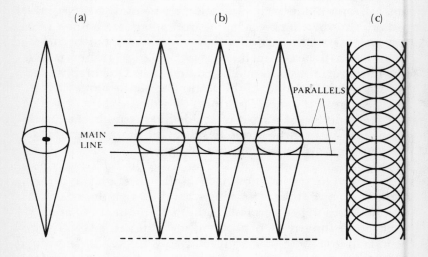

Figure 4.(a) Lethbridge's cones.
        (b) Development of wedge from cones on a line.
        (c) Formation of parallels from cone bases on a line.

mately at the same height as that of the male stone in spite of the fact that the base of the female cone is somewhat larger (radius 72.5 cm).

Underwood, in describing how the parallels of a water line are formed, published a figure which looks like a number of overlapping circles (Figure 4c). If these circles are interpreted as the bases of a number of overlapping cones, it is possible to suggest that a line is really an infinite number of overlapping cones lying side by side along the line which joins the centre of their bases. Thus, the field surrounding a line would then be a wedge rising above its base, with a similar wedge below (figure 4b). The parallels would then be the outer edges of the bases of the individual cones and should, therefore, be at a distance from the central line equal to the rate.

Now, on measuring the distance of the parallels of the central male line on the gallery above, I was surprised to find that these were larger than the widths at floor level and, moreover, that the angle of increase was approximately the same as that for the male stone previously measured. The conclusion was that I was dealing with an inverted wedge and that the actual line was situated in the air above the gallery level. I then made the assumption that the distance of the parallels from the central line was that of the rate, i.e. 60 cm for the male line and 72.5 cm for the two female side lines. If this was the case, the lines would appear to run just above the level of the eaves of the building. When I later found other lines at ground level I was able to confirm the distance of the parallels from the central triad was in fact the same as the rate.

These lines I had found in my stone-built church differed from all three of the geodetic lines described by Underwood. They seemed to be closely connected with the cones found above and below imprinted stones, and I formed the theory that they were the summation of all the forces of the stones making up the structure of the church. These stones must have received many blows with hammer and chisel when they were cut by the masons a hundred years ago, and during this process, became imprinted with the male rate in the same way as I had imprinted 'sling' stones. The female lines under the gallery were possibly a balancing force neutralizing the whole. I therefore decided to call these lines 'petrostats', to differentiate them from the three types of geodetic lines described by Underwood.

The explanation of lines as a series of closely overlapping cones does not, however, account for the phenomenon of blind springs. These appear to be about 1½ m in radius and always seem to occur at the terminus of a line. Although, as will be seen in the next chapter, blind springs form an essential ingredient of ley lines, I still find them difficult to explain.

Much of the work outlined in this chapter was described in a talk I gave to the British Society of Dowsers at their Spring Congress in Stirling in 1975.[15] After the talk one of the members asked in what way these lines I had described differed from ley lines. At that time I knew very little about ley lines, and I also thought that I was dealing with some form of aquastat. I therefore replied that, although my lines usually run straight, aquastats according to Underwood usually go in curves or zig-zags. I was probably right in my statement, but my answer to his question was really rather misleading. As it turned out after a great deal of further study, as described in this book, ley lines in their strictest form, are certainly a part of the petrostat complex.

In any event, I thought I had better find out something about these ley lines by first studying them in the field in the classic ley hunting style. Gradually I came to realize that with a study of these petrostats and other related lines of energy, it might be possible to shed some light on this mysterious phenomenon of ley lines.

2
Ley Hunting

As usual, Ethel produced the relevant literature. This proved to be Alfred Watkins' *The Old Straight Track*.[49] Watkins was, besides an expert photographer, a miller's representative, who spent much of his life travelling the countryside around Hereford in the early years of this century. He was very interested in the various antiquities he encountered on his travels and one day, when looking over the rolling country before him, he was inspired by the thought that many of these antiquities were sited on straight lines, to which he gave the name 'leys', running across the countryside. Later, when he checked this on the map, he found the idea appeared to be true. Much of the rest of his life was spent following up this theory.

The antiquities he found which conformed to the pattern were, besides standing stones and stone circles, prehistoric mounds, camp sites, pre-Reformation churches, castles, old wells, fords, and some old tracks. In certain cases, groups of trees, especially Caledonian Pines, seemed to be on these lines. Admittedly, not all these features could be considered to be of similar antiquity, but he pointed out, for instance, many early churches had been built on sacred sites of much greater age. His interests spread locally, and the Straight Track Club was formed, the members following up many of these lines in the field. By the time of the Second World War, interest had declined, but in the late 1960s and 1970s it had revived again, and now there are many workers engaged in mapping these lines and similar phenomena. A number of magazines and journals, such as *The Ley Hunter*, publish the results of this work.

The classical method of detecting a ley line is to examine a

map of the area, usually the 1:50,000, and mark on this any of
the features listed above that have been recorded by the
Ordnance Survey. Then, starting with a promising site, one
looks to see what other marked features are in alignment with
it. Generally, five such features within a distance of 25 miles
(40 km) are required before a true ley line can be suspected.
Field investigation is then necessary, usually with very
accurate compass work, although as will be seen later, this
may lead to errors because of the magnetic nature of such
sites. Accuracy is of great importance, particularly if dowsing
is not being used, because even on the largest scale map the
thinnest pencil line represents an area many metres wide, and
a map symbol such as a church covers a much greater area on
the map than does the actual building. Further, it is not
unknown for the position of a feature shown on the O.S. map
to be misleading (for example, standing stones could have
been moved from their original position). There are many
difficulties and uncertainties to be overcome, and Watkins
outlined some of these in his book *The Ley Hunter's Manual*. [50]
For the next two years I became an enthusiastic ley hunter. I
soon discovered that I could not use the classical methods
described above because, on examining the O.S. map of the
district, I could find virtually none of the necessary features
listed by Watkins. The sole exceptions were a few cairns that
might, or might not, be of ancient origin. I had, however, on
my local excursions found two obvious, but unrecorded,
standing stones, one at Arina on the North Applecross coast,
and, most conveniently, a small one of classic form on the
hillside about 100 metres above my house. As neither of these
was visible from the other, I had to devise my own techniques.
This is where my dowsing experience became useful.

To start with I walked round the stone above my house,
holding the Oasis Rod, and noted the exact points at which the
rod dipped. Using a theodolite placed over the centre of the
stone, the angles between true north and these suspected lines
were carefully measured. In fact, seven such lines were at that
time noted, radiating from this stone, three pairs being
opposite each other; in other words three lines passed through
the stone and one stopped at it. Later I found by very careful
dowsing, that the line running nearly north and south was, in
fact, a triple line, there being only just over 3° between each of
the three lines.

The next task was to find out where these lines went to. One was fairly obvious: to the north-west there is a gap in the hills on the horizon, and through this gap can be seen the crest of a small conical hill, which proved to be Meall Mor (Big Hill) at Fearnmore. I soon set off down the new coast road leading to Applecross, and checked with my Oasis Rod that a line did in fact pass over the top of this hill at the correct angle. There was no standing stone or cairn on the top of this hill, which was formed of bare flat rock, but I came to the conclusion that it was a perfect site for a beacon, which would be visible over a wide area in most directions. I later discovered that, standing by my home stone, which I called Rhu-na-Bidh (Point of the Pitch) Stone, the sun was seen to set exactly over Meall Mor on 1 May. I am not a sufficiently competent astronomer to know whether this would have been the case in megalithic days, but there are strong suggestions that this line was connected with the ancient festival of Beltane, when beacons were lit and various festive rituals carried out.

In the first edition I stated that this line continues out over the Sound to the north end of South Rona. That this is not the case was soon pointed out to me by one of my readers. In fact this line can be detected running out from the coast, but in the direction of Eilean Troddday off the north end of Skye. I have read somewhere that there are the ruins of an early Celtic monastry on this island, but cannot now find the reference, nor have I been able to check these facts on the ground itself.

Tracing this line back towards the south-east, I found that it appeared to run towards a notch (another of Watkins' features) on the eastern side of Ben Shieldaig, but, when I climbed up to this notch, I could find no line present. I had, however, discovered that I could locate a line even when I was some distance from it, by using a well-known dowsing technique. A short pendulum is held in one hand and the other arm extended; then, as one turns through a complete circle, the pendulum gyrates only when the extended arm is pointing towards the line, or object, being sought. Standing in the empty notch, I did this, and found that the line was more to the east. I moved about ten metres to the south and got a cross-bearing, which indicated that this energy centre was on the top of a small hill just to my east. Climbing this, I found that it was crowned with three boulders, each about two

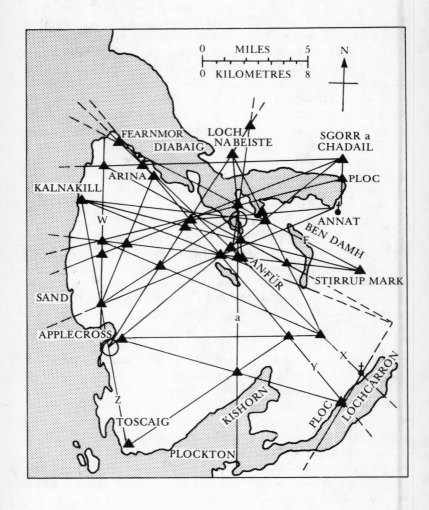

Figure 5. Principal ley lines found on Applecross Peninsula.

metres across. This was the centre I was seeking, and using my
Oasis Rod I soon found my line, as well as others radiating
from here. I called this important centre after Allt an Aoil, the
burn just below it. This line appeared to run on towards the
Stirrup Mark on the south end of Ben Damh. If extended it
emerges from the hills into Glen Carron at Coulags, where it
can be picked up again.

It must be made very clear that, at this stage of the
proceedings, these lines cannot be called ley lines; in fact they
can barely be considered as alignments, and are now known as
'dowsable energy lines' (see Glossary). As things proceed,
however, one finds these lines passing through more and
more features, where they cross other lines found in the same
way. Ultimately one gets to the stage when the places where
one has to make a field investigation are where three or more
lines cross at the same point. If these are substantiated on the
site, then one can consider them to be true ley centres.

The methods I had been using, i.e. plotting all the lines
round each centre I found, produced a considerable number
of such lines. The theoretical average of seven lines per centre
meant that their total increased by seven each time a new
centre was found. In practice it was not quite as bad as this, the
method being subject to the law of diminishing returns, since
more and more of these lines were found to run to centres I
had already located. In fact this method of ley hunting leads
inevitably to a complex matrix of interlocking lines which,
later in the book, I compare to a SPIN (a Segmented,
Polycentric, Integrated Network — see Glossary), rather than
to a single line with features strung along it, as is produced by
the standard method of ley hunting. In certain areas, particularly in those which had obviously been well-populated in
the past, as shown by the number of ruined crofts etc. (such as
the Shieldaig peninsula, as described in Chapter 9), the lines
were very dense and were therefore plotted on the 1:10,000
map. On this, a fine pencil line (Micrograph) 0.5mm wide,
represents a band on the ground only 5m wide and this is only
equal to about three times the actual width of the line and its
parallels. A 2mm circle marking the point of intersection on
the map is only 20m in diameter and if this can be accurately
located, it is usually clear which is the stone being sought; if
not, the pendulum will soon indicate which one it is.

The next lines to be checked were the closely adjoining

three running more or less north and south and crossing at the Rhu-na-Bidh Stone (see Figure 5). I had already noted a square stone lying on the top of a small headland about half-way down the peninsula, just beyond Camus Beithe (Bay of the Birch). The most westerly of these lines appeared to run in this direction, and I soon confirmed with my Oasis Rod that this was indeed the case. However, I found that the centre from which the lines radiated was not in the stone, but some 10cm from its side. Close inspection showed that the stone was lying on peat, which suggested that it had in fact been displaced from its original position, since the peat is generally considered to have been formed in the deteriorating climate after the Bronze Age.

This line goes on to cross the narrows between Loch Shieldaig and Loch Torridon and continues on the Diabaig side, where I again found it. Here it crosses a number of other lines, each crossing being marked by a large stone, and then reaches a stone on the far side of Loch-na-Beiste (Loch of the Beast). Jenkins [23] noted, when ley hunting in Argyle, that lines are often to be found in association with features named in the Gaelic after the Beast, the Horse and the Old Woman. My Loch-na-Beiste is a small deep lochan below a steep cliff and could be just the place to contain a water kelpie.

The central of the three lines from Rhu-na-Bidh first runs over a small hill, Cnoc Ruadh (Red Stone), where my wife found a standing stone of classic shape, but recumbent, and then also over to the Diabaig side. Many of the stones in this area are found to be recumbent, and I think this is because there is so very little soil or peat to set them upright into. The ground rock is usually so near the surface that nothing short of explosive would make a suitable hole to set an upright stone firmly.

The most easterly of these three lines goes on the Diabaig side to Loch Airidh nan Eachan (Loch of the Field of the Little Horse), again one of Jenkins' features. The stone here was of some interest, since it was in the shape of a dolmen, a flat stone about 2½m across, perched on the top of two smaller stones. Incidentally, this line running to Loch Airidh nan Eachan passes through a cairn on Sidhean Mor (Hill of the Fairies).

In the first edition I said that I had not been able to find on the map a feature named after the Old Woman (Cailleach) which Jenkins considered to be of great importance, since it was connected with the Old Religion and the White Goddess. Following publication, a reader called and pointed out that there was a Lochan Meall na Caillich marked on the limstone ridge above Loch Coultrie. On consulting my map of ley lines, I discovered that the one which passes through An Für, and which I describe later, appeared to go very close to this lochan so I thought I had better examine this more closely on the actual site. We made the mistake, fortunately as it turned out, of climbing on a very hot day, up from the Glasscnock side to the 1500 foot contour, only to find that the two little lochans were over the watershed on the Strathcarron side. Fortunately, as I say, because on looking up to the hill above me (Sgurr a'Gharaidh) I discovered the Old Woman herself (Plate 4). This, in the midday sunlight, looked just like the head and shoulders of an old woman lying on her back, and this is obviously the imporant feature, and not the two little lochans. A feature of this kind is not exceptional in the Highlands. If one looks up the glen from the village of Lochcarron, there is a hill (Fuar Tholl) which is locally known as the 'Duke of Wellington', there being a marked likeness to his profile in the shape of the ridge. When there is some snow on top, the Duke is said to be wearing his night-cap.

Checking the line with the Oasis Rod, I found that it ran along the ridge below the Sgurr. There was also another line which I picked up here and crosses the 142° line (Y), described later, at the burial cairn and spring on the limestone opposite Couldoran, and then goes on to Applecross. Since I was on the wrong side of the watershed, I was not able to locate the actual point at which these two lines crossed, but it appears to be very close to the two lochans. However, I had located the third Jenkins feature and was adequately compensated by my descent of the burn to Glasscnock, which falls 1500 feet in less than a mile, with frequent small waterfalls and many brilliant limestone flowers.

I did not at this stage see any direct connection between this feature and the other two mentioned above, but quite recently, while out cutting peats, I climbed up the south end of Ben Shieldaig ridge, above our peat bank. Here I found a small stone right on the end of the ridge, which the pendulum indicated was charged. As usual, it was not the first one I tested here; there was a fairly outstanding stone perched right on the edge, but as is so often the case, this was not the right one —

rather it was a smaller stone a few yards to the west. Checking on my ley map I discovered that this stone was on a line which ran from Loch-na-Beiste to the Allt Aoil stone at the north end of Ben Shieldaig and on to the Lochan-nan Caillich, thus connecting up the three Jenkins features.

I should here confess that I do not speak the Gaelic, which I find a most difficult language, owing to the complicated spelling and involved grammar. However, by browsing through Dwelly's *Dictionary*, which is really a Gaelic encyclopedia, one can usually deduce the probable meaning of a name. The Gaelic names, as with other Celtic languages, are usually descriptive, and if one translates them, interesting information about the site is often obtained.

I also traced the three lines passing through the Rhu-na-Bidh stone to the south, and again found features of interest. The one which comes from the Camus Beithe Stone goes on through the village to an early Bronze Age ring cairn. I had already discovered this and reported it, since there was danger of its destruction to make room for new council houses. (An official rescue excavation was carried out by archaeologists in the autumn of 1978 and the area now lies under the council houses' car park.) This line goes on to cross the head of Loch Shieldaig at a point where a neolithic flint knapping factory has been found, over an old well, and then up a valley in the hills to a large square stone where it crosses the 139° (X) line which I shall describe later.

The other two lines from Rhu-na-Bidh also cross the loch and I picked them up again on the ridge at about 380m above the sea. The central line (a) enters an area marked on the map as An Für, and here I found a most impressive stone perched on the very edge of the ridge overlooking the lochs. An Für, according to Dwelly's *Dictionary*, means 'welcome' or 'hospitality'. This seemed a most unlikely meaning for a rather bleak and inhospitable area of mountain top, and I wondered if perhaps the surveyor had mistaken this word for An Fhaire, which means the 'look-out' or 'guard point'. This at first seemed a very likely meaning, since from this point one gets a superb view of the Outer Loch Torridon, with Skye and the Outer Hebrides beyond. There are also some remains of the site of an ancient fort in this area. A still better view, however, is obtained from about a kilometre to the west, where there is a cairn, through which my third line passes. If anywhere, this should have been entitled An Fhaire, and I decided to refer this name to the cairn in the future.

However, I subsequently discovered that the name An Für for this site was not so incongruous as I had at first thought. A friend lent me a rather poor typescript (since lost) of a history of Applecross, and in this it was mentioned that there was an area of sanctuary within a radius of six miles round the ancient Celtic Abbey. I measured out this radius on the map, taking for the centre the old burial ground and cross, but it did not seem to pass through any of my features of interest. However, I later discovered that the Old Scottish Mile was 1984 yards, and if I used six of these miles as my radius, it just passed through the An Für Stone. If this stone was, in fact, marking the boundary of the sanctuary area, it could well be described as 'hospitable'. I also discovered several other ley centres on the northern part of this circle, with lines running like the spokes of a wheel, with Applecross as the hub. The southern part of this area is much less accessible, but I did find three standing stones in a line east of Toscaig, which may also be marking the boundary of this circle. The lines between the stones are, of course, straight, although together they make up a circle six miles in radius. Six Old Scots miles work out at just about 13,130 megalithic yards.[46] John Michell,[32] however, points out that one geomancer's mile equals 5,280 megalithic yards, so six Scots Miles are very nearly equal to 2½ geomancer's miles or 5,280 megalithic rods. This sanctuary area may, therefore, have a very ancient origin. However, when I came to examine the area around Applecross, I found that this solution was not nearly as simple as it had at first seemed. I will, therefore, deal with these difficulties later.

Just south of the An Für Stone the line crosses a small loch called Lochan Prapa on the O.S. map. As far as I can discover, there is no such word as Prapa in the Gaelic, but Dwelly gives Prabar as meaning 'the little people', perhaps a not insignificant meaning in this context. I wondered if this is perhaps another case of the surveyor having written down the sound of the word given him, without understanding the meaning. I have only dealt with three of the many lines on the Shieldaig peninsula, i.e. the ones running through the Rhu-na-Bidh Stone. Eventually I found many other lines in this area and I shall deal with the whole complex of them in full detail in Chapter 9.

One of the first standing stones I investigated was on the new
road to Applecross at Arina. (This is marked 'Arrina' on the
road, for some unknown reason, and according to Watson's
Place Names in Ross the full name should be Arinacrinachd,
which he thought may mean the 'Wood of the Druids'.) This is
a very clear stone about 1½m high, standing on the top of a
small hill just north of the new road. Amongst the lines I
found radiating from it were two with only just over 3° between them, running at 139° and 142° east of north and marked
X and Y on the map (Figure 5). There is also one running in the
direction of Applecross. During my later excursions I was able
to follow up both of these closely adjoining lines, and found
them to be of great interest. To the north-west the Y line passes
through the little township of Fearnmore, where there is a fine
standing stone sited between the houses. It then carries on out
to sea. There is no land in this direction for nearly 40 miles,
but on extending the line, it crosses the east coast of the Outer
Hebridean island of Lewis and then on to the great megalithic
complex of Callanish. I have not so far been able to check
whether this line is in fact detectable there.

Following these two lines to the south-east, they pass
through a pair of small and rather dilapidated cairns on
hillocks south-west of Fearnbeg. The 139° line passes over a
small mountain by the name of Meall a'Gharbhgair (Hill of
the Rough Ground), which looks as if it may have been
another beacon hill, and which is the meeting point of several
more lines, one of which starts at Loch Airidh nan Eachan and
then passes through Loch-na-Beiste. This 139° line then
passes through the cairn mentioned above, to which I had
given the name An Fhaire, and also the stone at An Für, and
then on to the Hill of the Old Lady, described above. On
continuing this line to the Lochcarron road in the standard
ley-hunting manner, I had thought that it might come out at
the church marked on the map. However, it was quite
definitely about half-a-mile to the west of this point. It only
occurred to me later that the church marked on the map is the
modern one and that the line was running to the ruin of the
Old Kirk and Burial Ground. I confirmed this later on the site,
and found that other lines also cross at this point.

This line raises two rather important points. Firstly, it is
generally held by many ley hunters that one feature in a line
must be visible from both the one before and the one after in

the line, otherwise they do not see how anyone as primitive as megalithic man could possibly be capable of setting out a straight line. They are, of course, disregarding the possibility that he could have used dowsing and also the possibility that an intervening feature could now be missing.

During my survey of the Shieldaig Peninsula, I checked line J (Figure 19)which runs from the Burial Cairn (17) in the village, over the top of Coire Buidhe to stone 8 on the other side, neither of which can be seen from the other. I traced this line most carefully all the way over the hill with the Oasis Rod, but could find no trace of an intervening marker stone on the top of the ridge, from which both other features could be seen. If there was one originally, it may have been removed.

The second point is, do ley lines run direct through the air from one feature to the next, or do they follow the contours of the intervening land? To settle this I spent some time examining the lines running from the stone behind my house (1 on Figure 19). Among other things, I found that these lines gave a reaction to the pendulum of either the male or the female rate, and usually changed from one to the other when they passed through the stone. Moreover, they were formed of triads, with further parallel triads some 60cm and 72.5cm on either side for the male and female lines respectively, just as I had found with the petrostats I had investigated inside my church building. Also, these parallel lines became closer to the central line when the ground was above or below the level of the stone from which they had originated. I was able to use this observation to discover whether ley lines travel at a uniform height over the intervening ground or travel direct from one stone to the next, irrespective or the irregularities of this ground. I found two adjoining lines running through this stone, one of which went to the burial cairn in the village almost at sea level, while the other went direct to the stone at An Für at an altitude of about 380m. Using the same techniques as I had used in the church to find the height of the petrostats there, described in the previous chapter, I found that the ley lines did in fact travel directly through the air from one centre to the next, irrespective of the contours of the intervening countryside.[16] There is, however, some very recent evidence [53] suggesting that energy lines may rise and fall at certain times, e.g. at the eclipses of the sun or moon, but this needed further investigation (see page 127).

Looking back now to the other line which passes through the stone at Arina, it passes just south of Meall a'Gharbhgair, where there is a fine cairn near the edge of Loch a'Mhuilinn (Loch of the Mill). How old this cairn is I do not know, but it is in excellent repair, and I noted that the lichens growing on it have spread from one stone to the next, covering the gaps. Lichens are very slow in growth, often adding only a few inches to their size in a hundred years, so this cairn may be of considerable age. This line then goes on to pass south of An Für and, where it crosses the three lines from the Rhu-na-Bidh Stone, I located small crossing stones. I was able to pick it up again just south of the road to Kishorn; here on the limestone ridge opposite Couldoran, I discovered a small burial cairn and a spring with a stone wall beside it; the line passed through both of these features.

Another line runs through this point from Meall na Caillich and goes on to Applecross, and a third starts here and carries on to the mouth of Glen Arr (Stag) just above the present Kishorn Oil Rig site. This obviously had to be checked, so my wife and I climbed up there recently and found that the stone was on a spur on the west side of the Russel burn and just south of the loch. This line continues to one of the three stones I had noted on the coast, south of Toscaig. Two other lines also run through this centre at Kishorn, one coming from the Ploc at Lochcarron, noted below, and then goes on to the Milton Stone at Applecross, which I shall discuss later. The third line appears to be the middle of the three lines coming from the Rhu-na-Bidh Stone and which runs through An Für, and to the south goes on in the direction of Plockton.

Returning to the line marked X on Figure 5, and which we left at the burial cairn opposite the Couldoran, it continues in the direction of Lochcarron, where it passes over the Ploc (a small peninsula) mentioned above, and on to the other side of the loch, up into the remote mountains south of Attadale.

Such Plocs seem to have been favoured by the megalithic linesmen and it might well be rewarding to do a little ley hunting around the village of Plockton, but this is rather outside my territory; it appears that the line which runs from An Für and through Glen Arr does continue in that direction. There is also a Ploc at Fasag at the eastern end of Loch Torridan and I discovered a line running over it and crossing others. This line crosses the loch to Annat (Mother Church) but does not, as might be expected, go to the site of the old chapel at the western end of the old burial ground, although this does lie on a ley line from the west. Instead it goes to a large flat stone about 2m in diameter at the eastern end of the burial ground. According to all the dowsers to whom I have shown this stone, it is not the site of a burial but does have a strong sacred influence, although one dowser said she found it very evil. Whatever its origin, this stone marks a ley centre where a number of lines cross.

Returning to the problem of the six mile sanctuary line, which I described earlier as being centred round the old Celtic Abbey; the site of this abbey is said to lie at the eastern end of the old burial ground at Applecross and there is a small stone building there which is reported to be the one remaining portion of this foundation. When I came to examine the Applecross area in detail, I found that none of the main ley lines ran to this site although there were some minor ones running from this building. The trouble was that, having lived in Yorkshire for so many years, I was subconsciously expecting something rather like Fountains or Rievaulx abbey, with a mass of geodetic lines, as described by Underwood, on the site. In reality, of course, this centre at Applecross was probably far more like the early foundation at Iona where there were a number of small separate cells for the monks, like the (still extant) cell of St Columba, and also a small central building to hold the altar etc. — which is possibly what the building still existing at Applecross is, although it does not look as old as the eighth century. Unfortunately, all the original stone has been removed, or incorporated in the modern chapel, so if present views of Underwood's theories are to be believed, the geodetic lines would have vanished along with these stones, leaving little or no trace of the original buildings.

One line from this building in the burial ground ran through the new plantation to the south and on to a large stone on a small hill just above the old mill loch at Milton, on the other side of Applecross bay. I found that many of the lines running into the Applecross area ran to this stone, a most impressive one about three metres high and wedged up with smaller ones below. In fact, one of the local inhabitants wondered 'how they ever managed to get it up there'. This stone almost certainly has a name in the Gaelic, but so far I have been unable to discover it.

There is a tradition that there was a stone circle somewhere at Applecross, but its actual location is no longer known. I had, however, noted some charged stones on a small hill south of Milton, and opposite the village hall, known locally in the Gaelic as the Hill of the Eagle. A dowsing friend said he thought that these stones were part of the circle. I therefore examined them with the Oasis Rod and found that there was indeed an energy line running through them and forming part of a circle, but the eastern third was over the edge of the hill and now missing. Possibly the circle had been complete at one time, but this side of the hill had eroded away. A line ran from here to the Milton Stone. There is a cairn marked on the map at the south end of this hill, just above Camusteel, but this is of very recent origin and not of any ley significance.

To the north of Applecross there is a line (marked W on Figure 5) running almost due north and south. Starting at Fearnmore, it runs through a prominent cairn on a hill west of the road and just north of Loch nan Eun (Loch of the Bird). After crossing the road near Cuag, it travels along a long ridge on which there are four or five small burial cairns, which are not marked on any map I have seen. It then goes on to a point not far from the old footpath which cuts across the hill from Sand to Applecross, well above the new road. It here crosses four other lines, one from the An Fhaire Cairn, another from the Burial Cairn at Shieldaig and one from Arina. The fourth comes from the debatable circle at Milton (marked Z on Figure 5), and on to the stone noted above at Toscaig. To the north, this line reaches the coast at Kalnakill, where it crosses one line from the Loch nan Eun Cairn and another from Meall a'Gharbhgair. I should add here that this cairn above Loch nan Eun certainly does not look very old, although it is the centre of a number of lines. I was told, however, by an old lady, who had lived most of her life in the area, that it was the tradition of the children, when out with the peat cutters, to add a stone or two to this cairn.

Of the various interpretations of Kalnakill (there is no K in the Gaelic alphabet), one is the Cell of St Coul, who was presumably one of the early Christian hermits, and I wondered whether the crossing of these lines was in any way connected with the saint's cell. Just north of this point is a cave

marked Uam an Triall (Cave of the Journey or Departure).
Since some of these caves round this coast were occupied in
the 'sixties by some 'Buddhists', I thought I should examine
this cave, but found it quite unsuitable for even the most
hardy hermit, being barely above the highest spring tides.
However, the Oasis Rod indicated a point in the hollow just
above the waterfall and here was a pile of stones in a spot
almost ideal for meditating far from the cares of the sinful
world.

Returning to the crossing of the four lines just north of the
Applecross path, this obviously had to be investigated on the
spot, so I set off along the old path to Sand and just in the right
position found a large stone which gave a strong reaction on
the Psionic Scale of 206. The stone was pointed on the north
side and flat on the south and gave the impression that it had
fallen over on its side. Further down the hill from this stone
was a fine grassy area on which Hut Circles and Old Shielings
were marked on the map and it was clear that it had been well-
populated in the past. It is not unusual in the Highlands for a
powerful stone to be set above a fertile inhabited site. I
remember travelling down Strath Naver in Sutherland, where
we found a fine fertile site with many 'larachs' (ruins) from hut
circles to roofless croft houses. On the hill just above was a
large powerful stone with many energy lines running to it. The
previous inhabitants may not have known what a ley line was,
but they were very capable of selecting a site for their dwellings
with a very favourable environment perhaps provided by this
stone.

It would seem therefore that there are two power centres,
one north and another just south of Applecross, which might
serve as the pivot of our circle of sanctuary. Unfortunately,
one is too far north and the other too far south for the circles
centred on them to fit the various features at the radius of six
Scots Miles. We have, therefore, to return to our first guess that
the centre really was the missing abbey. It would seem
possible that the founding father (Saint Maelrubha?) was well
aware of the pagan ley system, but considered neither of these
two Applecross power centres to be suitable for the foundation
of a Christian abbey, which he placed at the very fertile mouth
of the river Crossen. The circle was therefore likely to be of
Christian origin;they fixed it at six miles from the abbey and
found it was already well marked by the existing ley features.

I must make it quite clear that the lines and centres described in the chapter are far from the total that I discovered in this area, the greater numbers being in the more inhabited areas. This, particularly clear from the map of the Shieldaig area (Figure 19 on page 134), is dealt with in Chapter 9 where all lines and features are included. It is also apparent from the study of the north and west coasts of the Applecross peninsula where there are many small townships (although many are now deserted), as compared with the south coast where there is only one habitation between Toscaig and Kishorn and the ground inland of the single coastal path is extremely rugged. This must surely mean that the ley system was laid out where the ground was most suitable for habitation, and that it was treated in this way so that it would be more amenable for occupation. It was the prime purpose of my future work to discover just what this effect could be.

One day when I was out for a walk with a dowser friend, he drew my attention to four stones, set in the turf in a line behind an old croft ruin, each stone about 20cm across and set out 5 or 6m apart. His pendulum indicated that these stones were active, and my Oasis Rod showed that there was a line running through them, although this was not an area in which I believed there were any ley lines.

I thought a lot about this phenomenon when I got home, and decided to try an experiment. Having found part of the lawn in front of my house where the Oasis Rod indicated that there were no dowsable energy lines present, I set out four of my male-charged stones in a line, with about three metres between each stone. Testing with my Oasis Rod, I found a line, apparently similar to a ley line, running between them. Moreover, this line continued at each end beyond the outermost stones. These outer parts of the line were a complete mystery, since I had been careful to set out the line of stones so that it did not point at any nearby object on which it would be likely to attach itself.

I had apparently created my first 'ley line', and I quickly removed the stones so that this line could not possibly contaminate the environment. I decided, however, that this phenomenon must be investigated in much greater detail.

3
Measuring the Charge

Unfortunately, the existence of ley lines is not generally recognized by orthodox science, which requires that a phenomenon must be both measurable and repeatable if it is to be considered a part of reality, although this is, of course, no longer strictly true in the sub-atomic world. So far no physical instrument has been designed that will react to the energy thought to be transmitted along these lines or the charge in the stones, so it has not been possible to satisfy the first of these conditions. It has always seemed to me that this is no cause for denying their existence, since it may only be due to the ineptitude of the scientist in that he has not so far been clever enough to design a suitable apparatus.*

There are certain grounds for believing that Wilhelm Reich had gone a long way in his researches into this form of energy, which he called Orgone, and was well on the way to making such measurements.[44] Unfortunately, in the early 1940s, the public administration of the United States was not convinced of his claims, and most of his research papers were publicly burnt, he being thrown into prison where he died shortly after. Dr Don Robins [40] has recently published records of work done at the Rollright Stones in Oxfordshire, this study being part of the Dragon Project organised by *The Ley Hunter* magazine. He found marked activity in both ultrasound and certain atomic radiation, mostly at dawn at certain times of the year. This was mostly centred on the Kingstone, outside the main Stone Circle. The reason for these phenomena is not at present fully understood, but they are certainly something which should be more closely examined.

* See *Postscript*, p.162

It had occurred to me, when I was working on the dating of imprinted stones, [14] as described above, that I could possibly use the radius of gyration of the pendulum as a measurement of the energy thus stored in the stones. The big objection to this was that dowsing is considered by orthodox science, even when acknowledged to exist at all, to be a highly subjective phenomenon that is not repeatable. This, I am certain, is taking too strict a view of repeatability; it is one based on the nineteenth century dogma of the physical sciences that all factors other than the one being studied must be eliminated from the experiment, so that any reaction observed must have been caused by the one variant being examined.

During my career as an agricultural scientist I had been accustomed to carrying out experiments on crops in an environment that was quite outside my control. Indeed, experiments conducted in a strictly controlled environment, for example in a glass-house with uniform soil and weather conditions etc., would give little indication of the performance of the crop in the field. Thus it is of no use applying the treatment to one half of a field, leaving the other half untreated as a 'control', and then comparing the yields from the two halves of the crop; weather and soil conditions could have been quite different on either half and the difference in yield may not therefore be due to the treatment given. However, in the early years of the present century, fundamental pioneer work was done at Rothamsted Experimental Station by Professor R.A. Fisher on the techniques of statistical analysis, which was to lead to enormous advances in agricultural science.

Fisher showed that, if a field experiment was laid out on strictly controlled lines, usually in the form of random blocks within which each of the treatments was replicated, it was possible to analyse the resulting yields in such a way that the effects of each of the various factors affecting the yields could be separated. In fact, what one gets is a variation in yield for each treatment given in each block, and by the mathematical technique known as an Analysis of Variance, it is possible to assign what proportion of the variation in yield is due to such factors as soil differences, wind exposure, etc., as well as the treatments applied. When each of these assigned variances is subtracted from the total variance in yield, one is left with a residue known as Error, which is due to all the smaller factors affecting the crop that one has not been able to identify. Finally, one has to consider whether the effects of the treatments one has given to the crop are real or probably due to chance. This is done by comparing them with the residual error and expressing the ratio in terms of probability. What one accepts as real is purely subjective, but for agricultural experiments a probability of 1 in 20 (P=0.05) that the results are not due to chance is generally considered as satisfactory. This means that, if one advises twenty farmers to carry out such a treatment, one can reasonably expect nineteen of them to be successful. I have, however, on more than one occasion, had the difficult task of trying to convince the twentieth farmer, whom I had advised to follow my recommendations, that I was not totally incompetent and that he was merely unlucky!

Another most useful statistical technique which I was able to use in dowsing was the Analysis of Covariance. If one suspects that a factor A is varying with a second factor B, one plots these as a graph and tries to draw a line through the resulting points to illustrate this relationship. Assuming the resulting line is straight, one can, by subjecting the data to a Analysis of Covariance, find the best possible straight line that can be drawn through these points and estimate the probability that this relationship is real. The more mathematical reader will, of course, point out that the relationship may not be direct, i.e. represented by a straight line. It might, for example, be inverse or exponential. With experience, however, it is possible to make a guess as to the sort of relationship one is dealing with and apply what is known as a Transformation. Thus if the relationship is inverse, one uses the reciprocal of factor B, and if exponential, the logarithm.

There is one particular danger in using an Analysis of Covariance, and that is of assuming that because there is a significant correlation between factors A and B, variations in A are the cause of the variations in B. A good example of this was given by Nigel Balchin in his novel *The Small Back Room*. He describes a rather bored boffin with a calculating machine finding a correlation between the figures for the penetration of bullets on a firing range and the heights of the soldiers firing. Realizing that the heights could not have any direct effect on the penetration, he speculates as to the real cause, such that the air was more rarefied at the level of the taller soldiers, or, if they were lying down, that they were nearer the target—both equally unlikely causes of the differences. He had in fact realized that, although the two factors were certainly related, there must be some third factor, not shown in the data, to which both were also related. The discovery of a significant correlation must be examined with considerable circumspection before cause and effect are concluded as proved.

Using statistical techniques of this type, I found it was quite possible to use the 'unreliable' art of dowsing to make repeatable measurements to a degree of probability that would be quite acceptable, at least to an agricultural scientist. I very much doubt, however, if such a measuring technique would be acceptable to a hard-core physical scientist. More than once in my scientific career I have used an unorthodox method of measurement based on observation of biological reactions, only to have the research report rejected by the editor of a scientific journal on the grounds that the referees, to whom he had sent the typescript, considered the techniques used to be unreliable. This proved particularly irritating when similar findings were published perhaps some ten years later by another worker using a more 'physical' method evolved later.

I shall in fact be describing later in this book how I used a bioassay technique, with mustard and other seeds, to substantiate and check my dowsing. This type of technique is certainly not original in principle. It is frequently employed in both biology and medicine to assess the action of an agent when the process of that action is apparent but not clearly understood. One example is the assessment of the strength of a drug, by measuring its effect on colonies of bacteria etc. In my own branch of science, insecticides are commonly assayed by measuring the quantity required to kill 50 per cent of a batch of insects, the result being quoted as its LD50.

If I were to use the radius of gyration of the pendulum as a measure of the charge in these stones and lines, I had first to design some means of estimating accurately this radius. In the article in the *Journal of the British Society of Dowsers* [17] where I first outlined this work, I described and figured a 'gyrometer' for use in the field. Most of the work described in this book was, however, carried out in the more peaceful and stable atmosphere inside my former church, and a simple gyrometer was used. This consisted of a scale of centimetres marked on a strip of card, with 0 at the centre and 25 at each end. This was fixed about 15cm from the floor and with a beam of light focused on it. This needed to be virtually parallel, so a projector was arranged on the other side of the church. The stone or line to be measured was arranged to be about 20cm in front of the scale, and the pendulum was held over it so that the shadow of the bob was just below the scale on the card (Figure 6). As the pendulum gyrated, the shadow of the cord appeared to move back and forth over the scale, and when it had settled down to a steady rhythm, the radius of gyration could be read off the scale to the nearest half-centimetre.

I had already noticed that the longer the cord (rate) the larger the radius of gyration appeared to be. I therefore tried dividing each radius of gyration, as measured on this scale, by the length of the cord used, for a number of different materials, in each case using the appropriate Lethbridge rate.

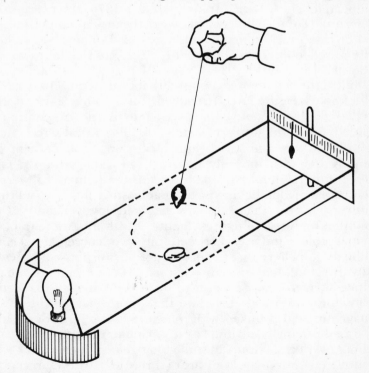

Figure 6. Gyrometer for measuring charge with a pendulum.

I found that whatever the material used, *at any one time*, I obtained the same figure for this ratio. I therefore called this the 'Standard Swing' (see Glossary). Unfortunately, I further discovered that if I repeated these measurements at another time, I obtained a different figure for this ratio. The problem was, therefore, to discover how this figure varied with time, and whether it could be predicted with any certainty. I need not confuse the general reader with the details of this enquiry, which I reported fully in an article in the *Journal of the British Society of Dowsers*[17] and which I have described in Appendix A. In short, I found that these variations were controlled by a factor which I called Psi ψ and which itself appears to vary with the phases of the moon and some form of daily rhythm, as shown in Figure 8A. Using these calculated values of Psi was therefore the method I used up to the time of writing the first edition of this book.

However, things were not quite as simple as they at first appeared. Thus when I started work in 1975, the maximum afternoon count at full and change of the moon was just under 140. Two years later it had risen to 160 and thereafter decreased to just over 100 in 1981, when it started to rise again to a level of 144 in 1984. Curiously enough the maximum count at the two quarter moons did not vary from 118 over all these years (Figure 7A). On showing this graph to a friend she remarked that this looked very similar to the plot of the annual variations in the number of sunspots. The Royal Greenwich Observatory at Herstmonceux Castle was kind enough to supply me with monthly figures from 1975 onwards. On inspection, I found that the means of the January to March figures seemed to be the most suitable, since it was about this time each year that I usually checked my psi-count. On plotting both sets of figures (Figure 7), I found there to be a remarkable similarity between the two curves. It seems difficult to believe that the occurence of sunspots could have any direct influence on my personal psi-count, but as I shall show later, this factor seems to be linked with geo-magnetic variations and it is well known that the reversal of the sun's magnetic field is linked with the eleven-year sunspot cycle.

I had originally attributed the circadian rhythm of the psi-count over the 24 hours to some biological influence, since so many functions of the body are of this type. However, recently I constructed a fairly sensitive magnetometer, principally with

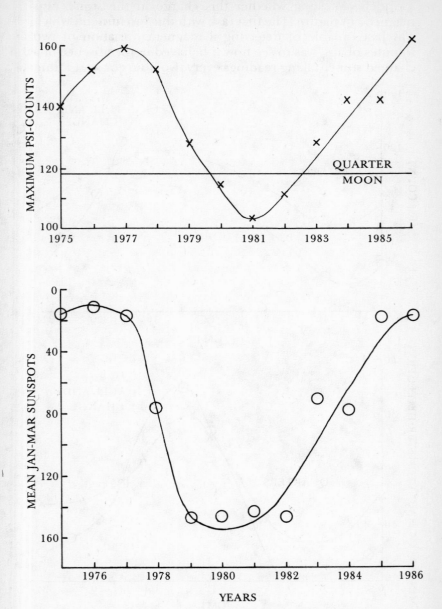

Figure 7. Comparison between maximum psi-counts and number of sunspots.

the idea of testing whether this charge in the stones was magnetic in nature. The first task with this instrument, which was just capable of detecting a magnetic variation of two minutes of arc, was to see how it behaved in the absence of a charged stone. Taking readings every two hours or so, I found

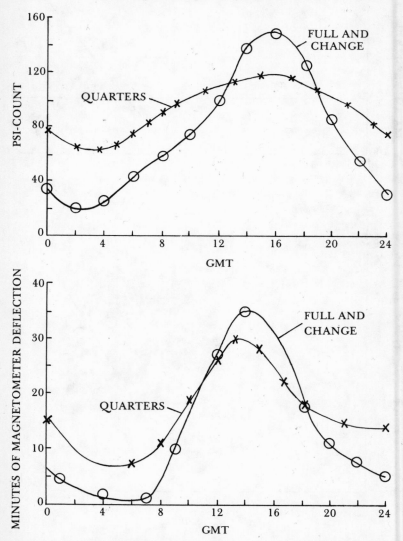

Figure 8. Relationship between daily psi counts and magnetometer deflections with phases of the moon.

that there was a deflection of over half a degree during the 24 hour period at full moon. These observations were repeated at the time of the quarter moon, when I found that the maximum deflection was only a little over 22 minutes of arc. Plotting these two curves (Figure 8) of daily deflections, I found a remarkable resemblance to the daily variations in my psi-count. Checking with such textbooks on geomagnetism as I could find [26] I discovered that variations in the earth's magnetic field of this type have been known for some time. They were originally thought to be due to the effects of the tides, since they are apparently linked with both the sun and the moon. This is, however, not now believed to be the case, since they do not coincide with tidal movements, as was shown by my own records. These variations are now thought to be the effects of the 'solar wind' which will be dealt with more fully in a later chapter.

This hypothesis that these two variations were both magnetic in nature obviously had to be checked. To do this I surrounded the gyrometer with an earthed fine-mesh wire netting screen, with the idea of shielding it from magnetic effects. I then measured the radius of gyration of a charged stone throughout a day when the moon was full and again when it was at the first quarter. The radius stayed quite constant throughout both the periods. It would appear therefore that the whole of these variations in the radius of gyration was due to external magnetic effects. Since I was standing outside the wire-netting while holding the pendulum, it is clear that any biological variation in my body could not be the cause of the variations. Recently, however, a correspondent pointed out that surrounding the gyrometer with wire-netting does not constitute a complete screen such as one would get with a Faraday Cage. However, it does seem to work in practice and it would appear that all my work over the years in determining an accurate value for the psi-factor in the equation for finding the true value of the charge on the stones was really quite unnecessary. Had I adequately screened the gyrometer from the effects of external magnetic fields, I would have been able to obtain a uniform figure for the charge at all times. However, by getting hold of the wrong end of the stick and then having to find out how to get to the right end, one often has to learn a great deal more about the real details of the position, with a consequent gain in real knowledge.

Having thus determined a reliable standard for comparison, I could now compare this with the radius of gyration observed (see Glossary) with the pendulum held over a charged stone, and I called the ratio of these two swings the 'charge' on that particular stone. This charge I measured in units which I called petrons (see Glossary). In practice I found that the charge ranged from around 20 petrons, where it was barely measurable with the pendulum, to a figure up to nearly 200 petrons. Detailed study over a large number of measurements indicated that I could obtain by this technique values which were likely to have an error of not more than ±3 per cent.

Later, I came across a rather different technique, known as the Psionic Scale. This was described by Reyner [39] and it is, I understand, widely used in psionic medicine. It relies on a comparison between the sample being measured and something having the same rate and of a known charge, this being known as the 'witness'. It uses the 'short' pendulum, and I have given full details of the technique in Appendix A2. It has certain advantages in that the equipment is readily portable and is thus useful in the field for measuring the charge on standing stones. Its main disadvantage is that unlike the gyrometer, it is progressively less accurate at the higher ranges of charge, e.g. over 100 petrons.

I was able to discuss these methods of quantitative measurement using the long and short pendulum with a philosopher friend and some rather interesting conclusions were reached. There seems to be good reason for believing that dowsing with the long pendulum may differ fundamentally from dowsing with the short pendulum. As I have mentioned before, when using the short pendulum one can only obtain the answers 'Yes/No/Don't know', and therefore to make quantitative measurements certain subterfuges have to be adopted. For example, if one wants to know the depth at which water occurs at a certain site, one has to ask such a question as 'Does it occur at over 450 feet?' Should the pendulum now oscillate indicating 'No', one then reduces the figure to, say, 400 feet and so on until the margin is small enough for one's purpose at this site. Thus the conscious mind is directing certain specific questions to the subconscious, which replies through the medium of the pendulum with the answers 'Yes' or 'No'.

Another method of questioning the short pendulum was

described by me when outlining my method of dating.[14] As I mentioned earlier, this used the binary notation of 'Yes or not yes'. Again, it is asking a specific question of 'Is this number, of which I am thinking (i.e. one of the binary series, 1, 2, 4, 8, etc.), a component of the date of this object?' and receiving an answer from the pendulum. But, because the total is not apparent to the conscious mind of the dowser until all the 'yes' numbers from this series have been added together at the end of the exercise, this technique is only marginally open to mental bias.

In use, the long pendulum differs from this in that the conscious mind is not really concerned in any way, and it would seem that the field around the object being dowsed is reacting on the reflexes of the hand and arm, causing the pendulum to gyrate when the cord is of the specific length for that field. Thus the stimulus to the sensory nerves passes directly to the motor nerves and muscles of the arm, without having to travel to the brain and back again. Thus, one can use the long pendulum when thinking about something entirely different, or even when the mind is blank. Indeed, it is better to do so, since it is only too easy to influence the pendulum's movement if one has a preconceived idea of the likely answer. If the action of the field is directly on the reflexes of the hand/ arm, the strength of this field controls the amplitude of the gyration of the pendulum, and a measurement of this can be utilized as a quantitative estimate of the field's strength.

It follows from all this that, strictly speaking, it is not possible to map dowse with the long pendulum, since it can only be influenced by a field in which it is actually operating. If one is map dowsing with the short pendulum, one concentrates on a certain point on the map and asks a question such as 'Is there water (etc.) at this point in the ground as indicated by this map?' One then obtains a 'Yes or 'No' answer from the pendulum. Should one hold a long pendulum with a cord of 75cm (the rate for water) over this point on the map, the pendulum will almost certainly gyrate, as it will over the rest of the map surface. The reason for this is that the rate for hydrogen is also 75cm and this element is contained in the cellulose of the paper. The pendulum will also gyrate over the entire map surface when being used with a length of 30 and 69cm, which are the rates for carbon and oxygen, and which are also to be found in the paper, therefore providing fields in which the pendulum is operating.

The fact that one is responding only to the elements in the fabric of the map would be demonstrated by trying to map dowse for the element magnesium which has a rate of 57.5cm. In this case nothing would happen. The pendulum would only gyrate if, by an unlucky chance, one were using a pendulum of 57.5cm as a short pendulum and asking the question 'Does magnesium occur at this point in the field as indicated on this map?' The pendulum would then gyrate only if this element did so occur. However, this is obviously not a true use of the long pendulum.

In spite of this, in a recent article A.V. Jones [24] described how he was able to measure the strength of blind springs when map dowsing, using a simplified version of my gyrometer. However, it appears that he used this with a short pendulum, i.e. of 14cm overall length, and not one adjusted to a specific rate.

This does not, therefore, contradict my contention that the long pendulum cannot be used for map dowsing. It is interesting to note from this that the short pendulum and its radius of gyration can be used at a distance from the field concerned and as a measure of the field strength.

All this would seem to indicate that as the short pendulum uses the conscious mind to interpret the reactions of the unconscious mind, much skill and experience is required in its use, and it is more liable than is the long pendulum to misinterpretation and conscious influence. The long pendulum, being entirely automatic, is thus probably more reliable for such quantitative studies as used in the work described in this book. No doubt I could have obtained the results hereafter described by using the short pendulum, but the time entailed would have been greatly extended and I feel sure that I would have had much greater difficulty in convincing the sceptics that the whole complex situation was not the product of a fertile imagination.

Readers of T.C. Lethbridge's books may well feel that this explanation of long pendulum dowsing is much more difficult to apply to his more abstract rates. However, such fields are certainly present when imprinted in a material object and can be readily detected with the pendulum set to the correct length; their strength can, indeed, be measured by the methods outlined here. When searching for a Standing

Stone, I usually use a pendulum with a cord length of 50cm, Lethbridge's rate for 'holy'; then only over a true Standing Stone will the pendulum gyrate and its radius of gyration give some indication of the charge in the stone. However, with later experience this seems to open to a rather different interpretation, as I shall describe later.

4
The Charge in Stones

I now had an acceptably repeatable means of measuring the charge, indicated by the pendulum, in both charged stones and also in the lines of energy between them. Since I had noticed earlier that such a line, apparently in all respects similar to a ley line, ran between two adjacent charged stones, it seemed a good idea that I should first investigate this charge in the stones before going on to study the lines between them.

To recapitulate what I had already found and outlined in Chapter 1, a stone could be charged by holding it in the hand and fixing this by hammering or throwing it hard at a neutral wall; but, if the stone was not handled, neither hammering or throwing imprinted a charge. Moreover, hammering an uncharged stone alongside one that was already charged imparted into it a similar charge. Having now the means of evaluating these charges, I was able to measure them on both the 'parent' and the 'daughter' stones, and found that they did not differ significantly, bearing in mind the error I was likely to encounter when using this measuring technique. For example, stone no. 6 had been heavily hammered in my hand and showed a charge of 122.2 petrons. On placing the unhandled stone no. 18 alongside stone 6 and hammering it in an area where I could detect no other charge, I found that stone 18 had acquired a charge of 120.5, i.e. well within the critical error of ± 9 per cent.

If a charge could be transferred by placing two stones together and then fixing it by hammering, how far apart could they be for this still to occur? To test this, I hammered a number of stones, each a little farther from the parent stone. From these I discovered that a similar charge was imparted to a stone as long as it was within a radius of 60cm round a male parent stone; outside this circle no charge was imparted from the parent stone. It will be recalled that Lethbridge had discovered that the base of the cone rising above a charged stone had a radius equal to that of the rate of the charge. From my experiments it was clear that any unhandled stone placed within this cone was becoming charged and this could be made permanent by hammering. To check this conclusion I repeated this experiment, but this time with a female-charged stone, and found that it transferred a similar charge to unhandled stones as long as they were within a radius of 72.5cm, i.e. the female rate.

If this charge existed only within the cone or field around a charged stone, was this also true of the wedge-shaped area of the parallels on either side of a line? It will be recalled from Chapter 1 that I had found a male line running down the centre of my church building with parallel lines on either side, and that these and the female lines at the side of the church did not run at floor level, the widest part of the wedge being at the height of the eaves. Only at this height were the parallels on either side of the main lines at a distance equal to the rate; at floor level they were somewhat closer. I had, therefore, to allow for this when placing my stones for hammering. A measurement of the strength of the male line with the gyrometer gave a figure of 120.5. I then placed an untouched stone just within the point where I believed the parallel to be, and another just outside this range. After hammering these stones, their charge was measured in the usual way, with the result that the stone which was within the parallels had a charge of 121.1 while that on the outside had no detectable charge. There was also the female line running down the sides under the edge of the gallery. I was, therefore, able to repeat this experiment with this line, and again found that only the stone hammered within the parallels received the charge.

These experiments indicated the useful fact that I had within the church certain areas where there was either a male or female line on which I could charge stones by placing them on or near it and hammering them to fix the charge. Also — and this was to prove very useful — there appeared to be neutral areas between these lines in the church where no charge was imparted to an unhandled stone. But, as will be seen later, matters were not quite as simple as they appeared to be at this time, and difficulties arose when I came to consider lines between stones and parts of the church wall. I shall be considering this particular problem in the church in a later chapter. It also appeared that the outside of the church walls had to carry no detectable charge, otherwise unhandled stones thrown at them would become charged. There was one other mystery: handled stones thrown at the wall received a charge that was fixed when they hit the wall, although they were outside my immediate field when this blow was received. This seemed to suggest that the charge received when handled was retained long enough, while travelling through the air from me to the wall, to become fixed in full on striking the wall.

It may be wondered how I managed to do all this without actually handling the stones. In fact, what I had done was to make a pair of long wooden tongs, which I always used for picking up stones which I did not wish to handle. This kept them well out of my personal field, and with a little practice I was able to use these tongs to throw stones at the church walls. At a later date I found an old pair of fire-tongs nearly three feet long and discovered that these were invaluable for moving stones about the place without handling them and thus imparting to them a charge. As will be described later, I found that to neither wood nor iron is it possible to impart a charge of this kind, so both pairs of tongs remained neutral even after long use.

To investigate this problem of stone-throwing, I handled a number of stones, immediately threw one of them at the church wall and then measured with the gyrometer the charge I had fixed in it. The other stones were kept in an uncharged area and then picked up with the tongs and thrown at the wall after various periods of time; the charges fixed in these stones were then measured in a similar manner. The charge found in each of these stones, expressed as a percentage of the full charge (i.e. that of the first stone), was then plotted against the time elapsed since handling. This showed that there was indeed a steady loss in charge, which appeared to be exponential in form. The percentage charge was therefore replotted, but this time against the logarithm of the time elapsed since handling, and now a good straight line was obtained. This indicated a half-life averaging just about three hours. In other words, after this period of time the charge would have dropped to 50 per cent of what it had been immediately after handling; after a further three hours it would have dropped to 25 per cent, and after 24 hours it would be less than 0.4 per cent; i.e. it would be quite undetectable with the gyrometer.

I wondered whether the length of time the stone was held in the hand had any effect on this decay time. I therefore carried round stones for periods of 5, 30, 60 and 120 minutes and then tested them in the same way for decay rates. I was surprised to find that none of this made the slightest difference and that the charge in each case still decayed at the same rate of 50 per cent in three hours. In desperation I carried this experiment to extreme lengths and carried a small stone in my pocket, where it was frequently handled, over a period of several weeks. However, on measuring the charge 24 hours after I had removed the stone from my pocket, and without touching it again, all detectable charge had disappeared. On the other hand, I have a small charged stone, in which the charge has not been fixed, and keep this in a tightly lidded tin. The full charge, as far as I can detect, still seems to be present.

I found it difficult to believe that blows with a hammer or against a neutral stone wall are the only means of fixing this charge into stones. I could hardly believe that the stones I had found charged on primitive graves (as described in Chapter 1) had all been beaten with a hammer or thrown on to the grave with some considerable force. I thought, therefore, that I had better look into this question of how the charge was fixed in stones.

My first attempt was to see if I could remove a charge already fixed in a stone by hammering. To do this, I charged a small stone and then measured the resulting charge with the gyrometer. I then placed this stone in my sitting-room fire, where it remained all night. In the morning the charge was again measured without handling and found to be the same as before. Having discovered that heat could not remove a charge already fixed in a stone, I now had to find out if it could fix a charge already implanted. To test this I collected three stones from the beach and handled all three of them. Stone A was hammered to fix the charge, stone B was placed in the fire and left there all night; and stone C was set aside and not handled further. The following morning, without handling any of these stones, I measured their charges with the gyrometer, finding that stone A and B had a charge of 151.4, while in stone C I could detect no charge whatever. Thus, if stone B had not been heated in the fire, its charge would have decayed, as it had done in stone C, hence proving that heating is an effective method of fixing the charge. It was not until quite recently that I realized that these experiments did not answer the most important question — does heating an unhandled stone impart a vital charge? To check this I therefore placed such a stone in the fire over night and next morning tested it with the pendulum at both the 60 and 72.5cm rates. There was no response. However, the pendulum did react at the rate of 50 — the rate for heat. This discovery will have to be considered in detail in a later chapter.

These experiments do, however, explain why there is usually a vital charge to be found in pottery, particularly if it is handmade, since the firing of the clay would fix the potter's field into the pottery. Machine-made ceramics are more variable, and this would seem to indicate that the period between handling and firing may have allowed the acquired charge to decay.

Aubrey Burl [9] and many other archaeologists have described finding the remains of cremated bodies at the base of standing stones, together with reddish soil indicating the heat caused by the cremation. There have been many and various suggestions as to why megalithic man carried out this practice, but the fact that heat fixed the charge on stone suggests a reason which at least is open to experimental testing.

If a corpse is simply buried at the base of standing stone it is clear that, if close enough, its charge will be imparted to the stone, but in time the body will decay, and, as shown in Chapter 1, the charge will ultimately be lost. Probably early megalithic man found that he could impart a charge to a standing stone by burying a body at its base, but being then ignorant of the technique for fixing this charge, he found that it gradually faded away, leaving the stone uncharged. Later, when he was familiar with the means of fixing the charge, he would have discovered that cremating a body at the base of the stone would fix the charge permanently in both the soil and the stone. Thus if he was using an unworked stone, to which no charge had been imparted by hammering, he would still have been able to obtain a permanent charge.

Heat as a means of fixing a charge also raises a rather interesting speculation. I have mentioned finding a number of centres when I was ley hunting, which had the appearance of being the sites of beacons where ceremonies at the feast of Beltane (1 May) may have taken place. Many writers have described how at these ceremonies, even in recent times, young men and women used to jump through the beacon fires which they had lit. Now, if it was desired to fix a vital charge into the rock at the top of a hill, one could obviously not stand near enough to the fire for this to be effective. As an alternative to burning some sacrifice at the stake, a field could be continuously passed over the fire, and thus be fixed in the rock by the heat generated by the beacon, without much danger to the participants.

While on the subject of folklore, it is interesting to speculate that the fixing of a charge by blows may be a possible explanation for the ancient custom of 'beating the parish bounds'. Writers have described how the priest and choirboys went round the parish boundary beating the ground with rods. (I believe that in some parishes this practice degenerated into beating the choirboys. Although this may well have been justified, it would not have any lasting effect on the parish boundaries.) Beating the ground would, however, fix the personal charge of the priest on the line and would, in times when most people were sensitive dowsers, be obvious to any interloper coming into the territory. This practice, therefore, closely resembles the habit of many animals marking out the boundaries of their territory with their urine or other scent. If the ground was stony rather than rocky, the charged stones would tend to become scattered during cultivation or building, and hence the line would have to be marked out again each year by the appropriate ceremony.

Dr Don Robins[41,42] has suggested that this property of stones to absorb some form of charge from an adjoining field may be due to the free electrons found in quartz rocks becoming fixed in the crystal lattice. I am not qualified fully to understand this theory, but it seemed to me that if it were correct, perhaps a magnet would fix a charge already imparted to a stone. I therefore placed a handled stone on a strong permanent magnet and left it there for three days. If the magnet was having no effect, the charge in the stone would have fully decayed by that time, so that it would no longer be detectable. On removing the stone, without further handling, I measured the charge, and was delighted to find that it was still fully present. Just to make sure, I measured it again after a period of some weeks and found the full charge still present. I thus had another method of fixing the charge into stones.

On thinking over all this, I wondered whether, if it could fix a charge, a magnet could perhaps induce one into an unhandled stone. I therefore placed an unhandled stone on my magnet and left it there for three days. On removing it, again without handling, I tested it with the pendulum and could detect no sign of a charge of either of the two vital rates. At that stage I was not in a position to decide whether or not there was a detectable charge at any other rate. Hence it would appear that the magnet can fix a vital charge already imparted into a stone, but it cannot impart a charge of this sort.

It has been pointed out to me that the three methods I had discovered for fixing the charge (hammering, heating and a magnetic field) are precisely those which are used for creating a permanent magnet in a piece of iron. This is, of course, not entirely coincidental, since, having discovered that hammering worked, I then thought of trying the other two methods. However, there is a difference in that it is a charge *already* imparted from some other source which is being fixed, i.e. rendered permanent, in the stone and not the creation of the magnetic field, as is the case with the iron. The parallel between the two processes is so close, however, that it suggests there must be some similarity in what is taking place, such as the re-arrangement of the molecules or electrons within the crystal lattice, as Robins suggests.

Whatever other means of fixing the charge in stones might be available, in this study I was using blows of a hammer, and it seemed desirable to assess the amount of force required to fix a full charge. So far, using stones averaging just over 100g in weight, I had been hitting them ten times fairly hard with the hammer. The force exerted by a hammer blow cannot, however, easily be measured or remain uniform over a long series. I decided, therefore, to use a stone of known weight dropped from a known height on to the specimen stone placed in a steady field, namely the central line in the church.

In the first series of this experiment I used specimen stones each weighing about 100g. One of these stones was hammered ten times and used to assess the full power of the field. On the remaining stones, another stone weighing 260g was dropped from heights of 5, 10, 20 and 30 inches respectively. The resulting charge fixed in each stone was then measured with the gyrometer, after allowing time for any excess charge to decay. The results showed that, for stones of this size, a weight of 260g had to be dropped from a height of about 28 inches to fix the full power of the field.

On considering these results, I realized that it was difficult to draw any general conclusion from this because the stone is not falling at a uniform speed but is accelerating. I therefore tried a second series, this time allowing the stone to fall from a uniform height of 38cm in each case and varying the number of blows. From this I gathered that a stone of 114g had to receive a minimum of four blows from a stone of 260g dropped from a height of 38cm in order to fix the full charge of the field. Did these figures hold for stones of greater weight? So far I had been using stones of little more than pebble size, whereas I was really interested in how a charge could be fixed in standing stones perhaps weighing up to a thousand or more times as much as my pebbles.

In my next experiment I used a heavier weight of 751g, dropped from a uniform height of 20cm, onto ten different stones with weights varying from 120g to just over 4.5kg, placed on the church central line. The charge fixed on each of these stones was measured with the gyrometer, and the results were plotted as percentages of the full charge of the field against the weight of the stone. This indicated that there was, in fact, a steady fall in the percentage of the full charge fixed as the weight of the stones increased.

The results of these experiments can be expressed in a number of ways, e.g. that the amount of work required to fix a charge of 120 petrons into a stone weighing 1kg is equivalent to 0.15kg. However, what we have to imagine is a megalithic stonemason sitting astride a lump of rock which he is trying to shape into a form suitable for a standing stone. He is doing this with the only means available to him — a stone hand-axe weighing, say 750g. Since the boulder is well within his personal field, how many times does he have to strike with the hand-axe from a height of, say, 25cm, to fix the full charge of his field into the completed stone?

To extrapolate the above results to a standing stone, we first have to know the approximate weight of the completed stone. Obviously, a direct measurement of the weight would be a task well outside my available equipment. If, however, the specific gravity of the stone and its approximate volume are known, the weight can be easily calculated. I remembered from my school physics lessons that all one had to do was to weight a sample of the stone in air and then again when immersed in water; on comparing the two weights one has a figure for the specific gravity. Nearly all standing stones in my locality are constructed from Torridonian Sandstone or Lewisian Gneiss. I therefore collected three samples of each, with differing grain sizes in case this affected the results, and weighed them in air and then in water, obtaining mean specific gravities of 2.599 for the Torridonian Sandstone and 2.499 for the Gneiss.

I decided to measure the standing stone lying just above my house, which happens to be of Lewisian Gneiss, but this proved to be no easy task owing to its peculiar shape. Although it is a typical pointed stone of four-sided cross-section, none of the four sides are of the same dimension, and the slope to the apex is not uniform. However, by taking plenty of measurements and doing some calculations, I decided that it has a volume of about 0.15 cubic metres. Multiplying this by the specific gravity of 2.499, I obtained a figure of about 375kg. From the data given above, it is clear that one would have to strike this stone some 428 times with a hand-axe of 750g to imprint the full charge of one's personal field. This standing stone is admittedly of a very modest size, if our mason had been exerting any extra degree of muscular power into his blows, it is clear that the work required to fix the charge would have been well inside the amount needed to shape this stone even if he had been very skilled as a stone-shaper.

The so-called 'lawn' of my garden has a number of large boulders in it, which tend to rise just above the general level of the surrounding grass, and form a considerable hazard to the mower. During warm summer afternoons I have often spent a few hours trying to reduce the tops of these boulders no more than an inch or two, using a steel bolster and two-pound hammer. Admittedly, my efforts are very unskilled compared with our hypothetical Stone Age mason, but I have found that it takes many blows to remove a most paltry amount of stone, even with this more sophisticated equipment.

When one considers the very large size of the Sarsen Stones at Stonehenge, which are, I believe, estimated to weigh up to 50 tonnes, one realizes that the amount of work entailed in shaping them to a roughly rectangular form, with mortise and tennon at the top shaped to receive the lintel stones, must have been enormous. On the other hand, it would have taken some 50,000 blows with a stone axe to fix fully the charge of the workers' fields. This sounds a great deal, but I have found that one can, with an easy rhythm, give one such blow per second; so the required number of blows could be given in just under fourteen hours' work. I cannot believe that these huge stones could have been shaped in such a short time as this with such primitive equipment.

An even larger stone is the grand Menhir Brisé at Carnac. The Thoms [46] describe this stone as having been about 70 feet high when it was upright and in one piece, and weighing about 300 tonnes. They suggest that it must have been cut from the solid rock by the making of trenches, 10-12 feet deep, with stone hammers, wedges, and water. Using the above data to calculate the work required to fix the charge of a worker's field into this immense stone, one gets a figure of 300,000 blows; at one per second, this represents a period of little over 83 man-hours, a quite trifling fraction of the physical work that it must have taken to cut this stone.

To check these ideas, I selected the largest boulder I could conveniently handle and weighed it on the bathroom scales — admittedly a rather crude method, but the best I could do with a stone of this size. I found that it weighed about 4st 6lbs (about 28kg). Using the hand-held axe weighing 750g, and beating it on the church central line, I calculated that it would require some 32 strokes to fix the full charge of about 130 petrons. If, however, I gave it the full 32 strokes — and this proved more than was actually required — I would still only get a figure for the full charge. I therefore decided to give it only 24 strokes to give an estimated 75 per cent of the full charge. At the same time I beat a small stone twelve times to give me a figure for the full charge of the line at the time of the experiment. This latter gave a figure of 133.9 petrons. Before the charge in the large stone could be measured, at least 24 hours had to elapse so that the excess charge picked up on the line could decay. I left it for three days and then measured the remaining charge with the gyrometer, getting a figure of 108.6 petrons or 81 per cent of the full charge. This would seem to indicate that I had been exerting some slight degree of muscular power in excess of a falling stone, and that a reasonable figure would have been one stroke of the hammer to fix the charge for each kilogramme of a standing stone.

Hammering, heat and an electromagnetic field may not, however, by the only means of fixing a charge in a standing stone. Early in 1977 I had been re-reading J.W. Dunne's

Figure 9. Dream scene of charging a standing stone.

Experiment with Time and kept a record of my dreams over a period of about three months. One night I had a very clear and unusual dream; I seemed to be standing on the left side of a valley running between rounded hills. At the head of this valley was a circular wall surrounding a tall, white stone, which somewhat resembled a lighthouse (Figure 9). Round the wall was a line of people dressed in what appeared to be early seventeenth century fashions, the men in short black tunics, rather baggy breeches and hose, white collars and tall hats; the women in long skirts, white shawls and caps. I had the impression, although I could not actually see anything, that they were passing something round in an anti-clockwise direction. There was a gap in the wall at the side facing down the valley and, after some time, something seemed to issue from this gap and rush down the valley with a sound rather like escaping steam or a sudden rush of wind. This rushed past me down the valley, although I could not actually see anything. At this point I woke up and recorded the dream in my diary.

I would not care to think what the Freudian interpretation of this dream might be, but my own explanation, for what it is worth, is that I had been witnessing a ceremony of charging a stone. The early seventeeth century was, of course, a time of considerable spread of witchcraft, particularly in Scotland, where it was much condemned by James VI in his *Daemonologie*. It is known that there was a ritual called 'raising the power', although I have no idea of the details of this. Could it possibly have been some method of raising the groups collective psi-count, and of in some way transferring this to the stone in the centre of the circular wall?

On re-reading Tom Graves' *Needles of Stone* [21] recently, it struck me that this dream was remarkably similar to his experience at the Rollright Stones, when he inadvertently opened the 'gate-latch' and let out the energy spinning round the circle. This energy, however, came out at a tangent to the circle and not radially as in my dream; but then the Rollright Stones do not, I believe, have a central stone, as my dream circle had.

To check the idea that the psi-count of a person was related to the charge imparted to a stone placed in their field, I hammered five stones in my hand, one every two hours on a day when there was a full moon, and measured their charges

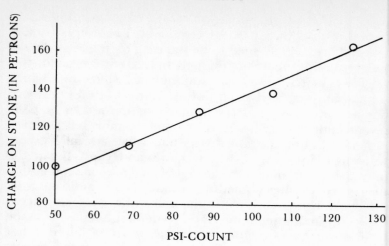

Figure 10. Effect of personal psi-count on the charge of a hand-held stone

with the gyrometer. The results are shown in Figure 10, where it will be seen that there is a good relationship between the charge fixed in these stones and the calculated value of my psi-count at the time when these stones were held in my hand and hammered.

It is of interest to note that the highest charge I was able to fix in a stone in this way was 162 petrons, and this was at the time of the full moon, a time notorious for witchcraft activity. Admittedly it was at 4 p.m. and not at midnight, as one might have expected. No doubt an experienced witch would be able to 'raise the power' to a much higher level than this; but this is the highest value I have been able to fix in a stone by means of my personal field. There is, however, an alternative and rather different interpretation of what I thought I was observing in this dream, and I shall deal with this in a later chapter.

Before leaving the subject of charging a single stone, there is one further aspect which must be considered. So far, I have been dealing solely with stones either of Torridonian Sandstone or Lewisian Gneiss, or very occasionally with Quartzite. I was interested to see what other materials could be induced to take up the vital male or female charge.

Lethbridge pointed out that most, if not all, organic materials, such as twigs and leaves from plants, or shells and bones from animals, already had their own sex charge inherent in them, and a further charge of different rate could not then be induced in them. Although my own observations on this aspect were far from extensive, I was able to confirm this. Man-made materials, such as plastics, have no inherent vital charge, nor can one be induced in them. Inorganic materials, such as metals, also have no vital charge, but such a charge can sometimes be induced in them in the same manner as I induced it into stones. It occurred to me that a possible explanation is that such inorganic materials are usually crystalline in structure, whereas plant and animal material is usually amorphous. Establishing whether or not such an explanation is sound needs far more investigation than I have been able to give it; it is anyway rather outside the scope of the present study, which is primarily concerned with the origin and nature of ley lines.

Another aspect of the vital charge, which was discussed by Lethbridge on a number of occasions, was the phenomenon of 'interrupters'. He found that certain materials, such as some forms of iron, graphite, common salt, and some woods such as elm and elderberry, had the property of 'masking' the vital charge in an adjoining material, or even changing its polarity. This is quite an intriguing phenomenon and, although I was able to use it when studying the lines of energy between stones, it is one which I have not yet been able to examine in any great depth.

5
Energy Lines and the Charge in Stones

After publishing the original edition of this book, I was disappointed to discover that this was the furthest point reached in it by a number of readers. They had taken one look at the rest of this chapter and decided that it was obviously the product of the 'Lunatic Fringe' and that the author was now trying to blind them with a mass of incomprehensible mathematics, which they certainly would not be able to understand. They would therefore read no more of this nonsense.

In writing this book, my intention was not only to interest the general reader, but also to convince the qualified scientist that ley lines were in fact a reality in which they should take an intelligent interest. On the whole I think I partly succeeded and partly failed. In revising the text for the second edition, I have therefore removed the whole of the mathematical argument used to explain the formation of these lines of energy, leaving only a simple statement of the conclusions reached. The more detailed argument I have transferred to Appendix B so that those interested and qualified to follow it may form a reasoned judgement of my conclusions.

From the previous chapter it is clear that I now had a fair idea of how, and why, stones become fixed with this mysterious charge, and it seemed to be time that I should start looking at the relationship between two adjoining stones and the resulting line of energy running between them when they were separated.

First, I thought I should try to understand what happened when two charged stones were placed side by side, i.e. what was the resulting charge when the distance between them was zero. I therefore gathered together a selection of stones with charges already fixed, varying in charge from about 20 to 160 petrons, and in weight from 70g to 4½kg. I selected two of these, placed them together, and then measured the combined charge with the gyrometer. This was repeated with a number of pairs of stones of various weights and charge.

Having collected a reasonable body of data, I tried to see if I could make any sense of it. I thought that one of three explanations might be possible: (a) the combined charge would be the sum of that of the two stones, although this seemed rather unlikely; (b) it would be the mean of the two; or (c) it would be something quite different and more complicated. On considering the results I had obtained so far, I was dismayed to find that it was clear that neither explanation (a) nor (b) would fit the case. The resulting charge certainly lay between those of the two stones concerned, but it tended to be nearer that of the larger stone; only when the two stones were of equal weight did the charge coincide with the mean.

Very briefly (the reader is referred to Appendix B (1) for a complete exposition) I discovered that the combined charge of two or more stones placed together was related to a factor obtained by multiplying the charge of each stone by its weight and I called this the 'power' of the stone. To obtain the combined charge of the stones one simply divided the sum of their powers by the sum of their weights, just as one would divide the power of a single stone by its weight to obtain a figure for its charge. I decided to call each 100 units of power one 'lithon' to differentiate it from the units of charge which I had called petrons (see Glossary). Thus a stone weighing 1kg and having a charge of 100 petrons would be said to have a power of 1 lithon.

I was now able to calculate a charge for the two stones together and compare this with the result I had obtained with the gyrometer and pendulum. This I did and found that the calculated charge certainly related very well with the observed one, except that it was always about 10 per cent less. I was quite unable at this stage to see any reason for this discrepancy and went on measuring pairs of stones and calculating their theoretical combined charge for a period of about three months without any further elucidation. In fact it was not until after the publication of the first edition that the true explanation became apparent.

In desperation I finally got tired of this and decided to go on to the next stage without solving this problem, using the calculated figure for the charge at zero separation rather than that actually measured. This next stage was, in fact, to move the two stones apart and see what was the 'strength' of the line between them at various distances of separation. I decided to call this the strength of the line rather than the charge, which did not seem to be very appropriate for a line. This strength was, however, being measured in the same way as was the charge, i.e. with the gyrometer, so rightly or wrongly, I stuck to the same units of petrons.

Prior to starting work on the paired stones I had been doing most of this work in the vestry, a small room about nine feet square at the north-west end of the church. I now had to have more room to spread out my two stones; so I moved on to the eastern gallery of the church. I had already checked that there were no detectable lines on this gallery, and it gave me a stretch of more than fifty feet to spread out my stones. I therefore set up two stones about twenty feet apart on this gallery and duly checked with both pendulum and Oasis Rod that there was, indeed, a line between them. I then tested the space between each end wall and the nearest stone, and was discouraged to find that there was a line here also. There had been no line between these walls before, but when I set up these two stones, a line appeared from wall to wall. I then recalled the experiment I had tried at the outset of this work, namely setting up four stones in the garden and finding a line between them as well as a weak line running out from each end-stone. It would appear that, when one sets up a line between two stones, this line continues and 'latches' on to the nearest suitable objects, e.g. some charged stone.

I thought I had better check this suggestion and see what would happen if there was no suitable target for the line to latch on to. Looking out to the north-west from the Rhu-na-Bidh point over Loch Shieldaig, there is a gap about 1km wide between the points of Ardheslaig and Diabaig. To the left of this gap, the tops of the hills of Harris and South Lewis, some fifty miles away, can be seen on a clear day, but to the right of the gap all land is below the sea horizon. On the point of Rhu-na-Bidh I set out two stones, each of about 1½kg in weight, with a charge of 120 and 114 respectively. The seaward stone was about 1m from the edge of the cliff, and the other about 6m further inland. The line between them was carefully sited to run on to the horizon where no land was to be seen. Between the stones was a line with a strength of just over 100 petrons as measured with the portable gyrometer, and inland, a line of 52 petrons. I could detect nothing with the pendulum on the seaward side. I then moved the inland stone so that the line was now pointing to the highest part of the Ardheslaig peninsula, which is about 4 km distant. I could now just detect a line on the seaward side with a swing of the pendulum of only 2cm radius, indicating a strength of 17.5 petrons. I am not sure what features there may be on the Ardheslaig peninsula, since I have not yet surveyed it, but I do know that several ley lines run out in its direction, and there are in all probability several standing stones in that area.

All this seemed to show that, if one sets up a line between two stones, the line will extend at both ends when there is something suitable to latch on to. With my line which I had set up on the gallery of the church, the end walls were forming a suitable target. As I stated above, I had been unable to detect any line running along the gallery *before* I had placed the two stones there, and I had assumed wrongly that the walls were not charged, especially as I had picked up no charge when throwing stones at the outside. This conclusion must surely have been wrong, since the outside of the church wall is constructed of square cut stones, which would have picked up a charge from the masons shaping them. On the other hand, the inner part of the walls, which are over a metre thick, is formed of mortar and rubble which would not be charged. The charge of the cut stones would, therefore, have to be shared with the rubble, considerably reducing the overall power. The interesting point is that the only indication of this charge was the male and female lines running down the length of the inside of the church, as I have previously described. We shall consider this problem in more detail in a later chapter.

Whatever the reason for all this, I had to find some means of isolating my two-stone line so that it was not interfered with by the power of the church walls. Migrating to the garden would not help, because I would find the line latching on to all kinds of unknown objects in the environment. My mind therefore turned to Lethbridge's interrupters, mentioned in the last chapter. I wondered whether a sheet of iron placed at each end of the gallery might stop the church interfering. I collected a pair of old tin trays, placed one at either end of the gallery, and again set up my two stones. The reader can imagine my relief when I could detect no line between these stones and the church walls, only that between the two stones.

After some thought I wondered if this interference by the church walls was the cause of my previous trouble with the combined charge of two stones at zero separation. I thought, therefore, I would try measuring this joint charge with two stones isolated from external effects. I had in the meantime found that fine gauge (30mm or less) wire netting was just as good a screen as a sheet of iron; so I surrounded my two stones with this at a distance of about 1m and again measured the joint charge. On comparing this with the figure I had obtained with unscreened stones, I found a reduction of about 8.8 per cent. I repeated this with other pairs of stones and found very similar figures for the reduction in charge. The interference had thus been the reason for the trouble I had encountered when comparing the observed charge with that calculated, and I could therefore accept my original hypothesis that this, indeed, represented the correct charge when two stones are placed together. No doubt the reader will immediately ask: 'If this interference had been causing me to overestimate the charge in pairs of stones, what about all the single stones I had been measuring over the years?' Very true, but it must be remembered that although I did not at that time realize that it was the variations in the magnetic field which was upsetting my measurements, I had been compensating for this by the use of the psi-factor. It would appear that this was just what was happening with my measurements of the combined charge of two adjoining stones, and this was removed when I adequately screened the area where I was carrying out these measurements.

With our knowledge of how the charge of two adjoining stones is made up, we can consider the implications of this finding. Firstly, what is the effect of placing an uncharged stone alongside a charged one? We can now see that it depends on their relative masses. Since one of the stones is uncharged, it follows that its power is zero, and if its mass is very small compared with that of the charged stone, the result will simply be the charge of the large stone alone, and both stones will then have the same charge. This is, in practice, quite a useful conclusion, because it means that one can measure the charge of a Standing Stone simply by hammering a small stone (e.g. of about 100g) alongside, and then measure this with the gyrometer at one's leisure. It is often not very easy to balance the gyrometer on the top of a pointed Standing Stone in a gale!

Secondly, we have to consider the case of when we are dealing with a large pile of stones, each of different masses and possibly having different charges. The overall charge is then made up of the sum of their individual powers divided by the total mass. To confirm this, one would, of course, have to dismantle the cairn and then weigh and measure the charge on each individual stone — not a very feasible proposition. But it does mean that to measure the power of a cairn, if one can get a rough estimate of its mass, then one only has to multiply this by the overall charge as determined from a small stone hammered alongside.

It is also of interest to consider what happens when one places a small, highly-charged stone alongside a large, uncharged one. It is clear from what I have said that the larger mass of the second stone is now the important factor, and that the resulting charge on it will be much less than that of the smaller stone. I tried out this combination, mainly to see if there would be any lasting effect on the smaller stone after it had imparted a charge to the larger one. My first attempts were not very successful, because I had chosen an uncharged stone which was much too large, with the result that the combined charge was too small to measure with the gyrometer. At my third attempt, using a small stone weighing only 72g, I got a combined charge in the large stone of 33.6, whereas the calculated charge was only just larger than this at 36.7 petrons.

The interesting point of this experiment is that even after three attempts, I could detect no reduction in charge in the smaller stone. This is, of course, rather obvious and bears out what might be termed the 'Lethbridge principle of conservation of charge', namely that once a stone has been given a fixed charge, it remains in it for all time. Obviously, if it lost some of its charge to every stray stone that happened to come into its field, its charge would be very rapidly depleted. As I have already mentioned, I have a stone arrowhead which must be all of four thousand years old but which still has a strong male charge. (This charge could, of course, have been acquired at a later date, but the original act of knapping would certainly give it such a charge.)

I now seemed to have enough information to start working out what happens when one moves the two stones apart. I therefore set up two stones with a combined power of 9.08 lithons on the gallery of the church, where I had just enough room to move them as far apart as 53 feet. I then marked out stations at 0, 13, 23, 33, 43, and 53 feet, and placed a tin tray at either end of the line to screen any influence from the building. (It may well be wondered why I suddenly reverted to the use of feet here, having used metric units in most other experiments. The truth is that my steel tape is graduated in feet, and it was easier to use this and to convert my results to metres at a later stage.) The strength of the line between the two stones was measured with the gyrometer, moving one of these stones to each of these stations in turn, the other stone remaining stationary. This process was repeated three times, about two or three hours intervening between each series, so that any changes in psi could be allowed for, although it was realized later that this was unnecessary since the line was now being screened from any outside influences. The mean

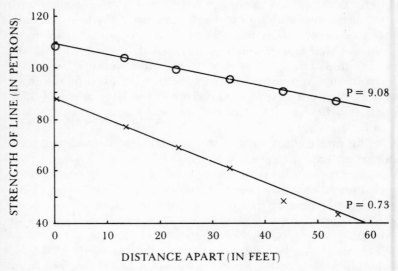

Figure 11. Reduction in strength of line between two stones at various distances.

strength of the line in petrons was worked out for each station and the results plotted against the distance (Figure 11). The whole procedure was then repeated, but this time with two stones having a joint power of 0.73 lithons, and the results plotted on the same graph.

It will be seen clearly from this graph that the fall in strength of the line running between the stones was proportional to the distance of separation, and also that the *rate* of this decrease was greater with the pair having the smaller power than it was with the other pair of stones. This had, therefore, to be looked at in more detail. I also noticed from this graph that both lines passed through the zero value for separation at the calculated values rather than those measured when the pair were unscreened. I was, therefore, right in using this figure rather than that obtained with unscreened stones.

What I now had to do was to see how this rate of decline in strength on increasing distance varied with differences in the combined power of the pairs of stones. I did this by measuring the rate of decline for twelve pairs of stones, each pair having a different combined power. The results of this work were then plotted against the combined power. (This is dealt with in detail in Appendix B (2) together with the equation I managed to derive from them.) In simple words, this meant that if the weight and charge of the two stones is known, it is possible to calculate with quite reasonable accuracy the strength of the connecting line, whatever the distance that separates them.

Does this equation make sense if applied to two standing stones, each weighing 1 tonne, with a charge of 100 petrons each? They would thus have a joint power of 2000 lithons, and if separated by a distance of 1km, the reducation in the zero separation strength of 100 petrons would be just 9.15 per cent, giving a line strength of 90.85 petrons — which seems quite reasonable. Two stones in a line do not, however, make a classical ley line, so I now had to go on to see what would happen if I added a third stone to the pairs already used. Again I managed to produce an equation (see Appendix B (3)) which showed that in adding a third stone the strength of the line between my original pair had been increased.

This final relationship can, however, be considered as a unique situation, since I had used only one value (111.3) for the strength of the line between my fixed-distance line. To investigate the complete relationship, the whole experiment should have been repeated at least a dozen times, with stones and lines of different values, in order to get a reasonable set of figures for consideration. However, this one experiment alone had entailed making 120 measurements with the gyrometer, and I did not feel inclined to repeat it twelve times, especially as my next investigation showed that the situation was even more involved than it had so far proved to be. It soon emerged, of course, that any attempt to formulate an overall relationship would prove exceedingly complex.

Thinking over how the situation, as known so far, could be applied to standing stones and ley lines in the field, I recalled that no natural standing stone had a single energy line running through it, as had my experimental stones. Most of them seemed to have three, plus one which ended (or started) there. If adjoining sectors of a line had such an effect on each other, as I had found, could the other two lines passing through the stone at an angle also have an effect on it? To test this, I set up two stones (Nos 21 and 11) in line on the gallery, twenty three feet apart, *without* screens at either end, so that I had a continuous line from wall to wall. The strength of the line between these two stones was then measured, and proved to be 105.8 petrons. Two other stones were then set up at 4 and 6 feet on either side of stone No. 11, so that the line between them was at right-angles to the previous line passing through stone 11. The line between stones 21 and 11 was then measured again with the gyrometer and now proved to be 123.7 petrons. Next I measured the strength of the crossing line and found this to be 127.1. I then repeated the whole procedure with two much smaller stones on the crossing line, these having a line between them of only 71.9, and found that now the strength of the line between 21 and 11 was only 83.8. In other words, in crossing my original line of 105.8 petrons by another of greater strength, I had increased its value, but when the crossing line was weaker, the original line had been reduced in strength.

Standing stones, as I pointed out in Chapter 2, usually have an odd number of ley lines, i.e. one line ends (or starts) at the stone and does not run through to form another line on the other side. Does this truncated line have a similar influence on the remaining lines as does a line passing right through, as discussed above? To test this, I set up the same experiment, with stones Nos 21 and 11, 20 feet apart, but, instead of having two stones opposite stone 11, I had this time only one, 6 feet away, with a tin tray on the other side to prevent the line travelling on to the church wall. I then measured again the strength of the line between stones 21 and 11 and found that this time it had been raised to 117.6 petrons, i.e. not so much as when the two stones had been opposite it, but still quite an appreciable degree of increase.

A possible explanation of this apparently complex situation may be that a line arriving at a stone modifies its 'effective' charge. Thus its power would then be altered and this would in turn modify all the other lines running to that stone. This would be a most complex model, quite beyond my limited means to substantiate.

One further aspect had to be looked into: standing stones can have a female (negative?) charge, with the pendulum reacting to a rate of 72.5cm, although in my experience of the stones and cairns in this area, most of them appear to be male. Would this female charge affect my calculations of power and strength? I set up two female stones, of known weight and charge, 20 feet apart and measured the strength of the line between them, but this time with a pendulum of 72.5cm. This strength worked out at 84.6 petrons. I then calculated the theoretical strength, using equation A (9), and this came to 84.3 petrons — a figure quite surprisingly close. This experiment was then repeated , but using a female stone at one end a male one at the other. Measurements this time came to 96.9, with a calculated figure of 92.9. These last measurements were made with both the 60cm and 72.5cm pendulum, but this made no difference when this factor was allowed for in the calculations. It was clear, therefore, that, even if the charge in two adjoining standing stones is of opposite 'polarity', equation A (9) holds good for calculating the strength of the line between them. This and other facts do not seem to support the idea that the male and female charges are really of opposite polarity. This will have to be discussed in greater detail in a later chapter.

Despite my success in being able to calculate the strength of a line between two stones, my idea of being able to go out into the countryside and find two adjoining standing stones, measure their size and charge, then with a few quick stabs at my pocket calculator predict the strength of the line between them, was obviously no more than a pipe-dream. Such a line would be modified by the powers of all the other stones and lines in the area. Even if this intricate complex could be determined, any variation in one would at once affect all the other stones and lines in the area.

In spite of this, I decided that I really ought to check my findings in the real world, since so far I had been working with little more than pebbles when they were compared with standing stones. I had already worked out the size and approximate weight of the Rhu-na-Bidh stone and the Square Stone of Camus Beithe, and I knew that they were approximately 750m apart. I now set out to measure the charge on each of these stones and the strength of the line between them. For convenience I did this by hammering small stones, each of about 100g, on these two standing stones. Strictly speaking, the strength of the line between them should have been measured at each end at the same moment in case there was any variation in strength during the twenty minutes it took me to walk from one stone to the other. However, as there was only about 1 per cent difference in the two values obtained at either end, it is clear that the line had not changed appreciably during this interval. For good measure, I also hammered stones on the lines extending beyond the two stones. The values obtained for the various strengths are shown in Figure 12, together with the calculated power of each stone. Since the weights of the stones were known (374 and 960kg), it was

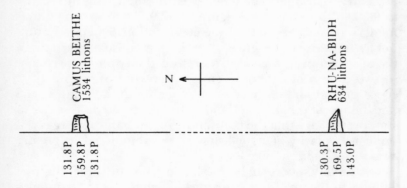

Figure 12. Strength of ley line between Rhu-na-Bidh and Camus Beithe standing stones.

possible to work out the theoretical strength of the line between them *had they been screened from outside influences*. This worked out at 152.7 petrons, a figure rather higher than the 131 obtained by measuring. But, of course, I did not know what the effect of the other lines and stones in the area might be. The line running north from the Camus Beithe Stone, as will be seen from Figure 12, had just about the same value as this, but I do not know what the next stone in that direction may be, because it here crosses the Loch to the Diabaig side. Running south, the line is stronger; it runs to the site of the burial cairn in the village, but there is, to my knowledge, at least one small crossing stone in between. Taking all this into consideration, it seemed that my extrapolation from pebbles to standing stones was not too wildly out.

Up to this stage in my researches, I had only been using stones charged at the male and female rates, mainly using Torridonian Sandstone. However, late in 1984 I was staying with friends in Yorkshire and discussing my work with their son and his wife, who lived at Prescelly, South Wales. I mentioned that I had always wondered why megalithic man had gone to such immense trouble to bring large lumps of Bluestone, weighing up to four tonnes [1] all the way from Prescelly to erect them at Stonehenge. What was so very special about this particular stone?

Just before Christmas, a small but heavy parcel arrived for me. On opening it, I discovered that they had sent me a sample of this mysterious stone. It was certainly slightly blue in colour, with spots of white scattered through it; geologists describe it as 'prescellite' or 'spotted dolerite'. The spots of white in it can be clearly seen and are of quartz. On testing this stone with my pendulum, I found that it reacted at a rate of 50 but not at 60, in spite of the fact that I had just been handling it. This was, no doubt, due to the presence of the spots of quartz in this stone, since this material is a powerful interrupter and would have masked my personal field rate of 60. There is a certain amount of plain dolerite, lacking the quartz spots, in the Shieldaig area, and some of the stones in my garden wall are of this material; it is, however, more black in colour than blue. Lacking the quartz spots found in the Bluestone, this dolerite will take a male charge when held in the hand, but the pendulum also reacts to the rate of 50 in the same way.

These two minerals are classified by geologists as igneous, and are commonly found in the faults of other rocks, having welled up from below when in a molten state. This partly explains the reaction of the pendulum to the rate of 50, since this is the one which Lethbridge gives for heat. It will be shown later, however, that this rate also indicates that rocks of this type have a residual magnetic field which is of great importance when considering our subject of ley lines.

It must here be made very clear that an inherent charge of a material is not transferable to another substance, even when hammered in each other's fields. Thus placing a stone on a sheet of copper and hammering with an iron hammer does not transfer the rates for copper (76) or iron (80) to the stone. In the same way it is not possible to transfer the residual magnetic charge found in an igenous rock such as Bluestone at normal room temperatures, but this may be possible at a much higher temperature. However, it was found that an energy line flowed between this Bluestone and a piece of dolerite, and also between two pieces of quartz.

Plate 1. The Rhu-na-Bidh Stone from the author's garden.

Plate 2. Loch-na-Beiste looking east. The ley line crosses the centre of the loch to a standing stone above the cliff to the left.

Plate 3. Dolmen stones by Loch-Airdh-nan-Eachan.

Plate 4. Hill of the Old Woman (Cailleach).

Plate 5. An Für standing stone overlooking Loch Shieldaig.

Plate 6. An Faire Cairn overlooking Loch Shieldaig.

Plate 7. Position of missing stone at Ob Mheallaidh.

Plate 8. Bioassay of stone charge. The stones and pots of mustard seed are placed inside the open tins. The figures indicate the charge.

Plate 9. Two methods of conducting a bioassay.

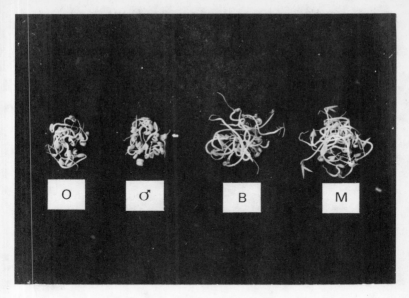

Plate 10. **Effect of treated water on Mung Beans**
O = Untreated.   ♂ = Male charge.
B = Bluestone.   M = Magnet.

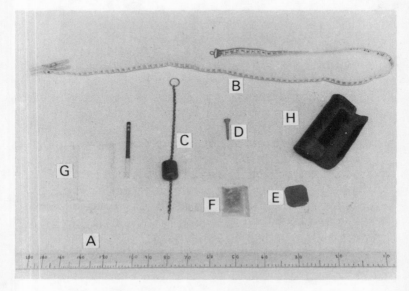

Plate 11. **Equipment for using the Psionic Scale.**

Plate 12. Using the portable gyrometer.

6
Charged Stones and Plant Growth

Many writers have suggested that ley energy might have been collected and used to encourage fertility in crops and domestic animals. Underwood [48] noted that mistletoe, crow garlic (*Allium vinealis*) and various trees such as yew, hawthorn, hazel and apple, were all apparently affected by geodetic lines, often showing twisted growth when growing over blind springs etc. Maby and Franklin [31] in their study of the physics of dowsing, found that many plants were affected in one way or another when they were growing over the underground streams they had detected by dowsing. I therefore thought it was important to see if my charged stones had any effects on plant growth and germination.

This test was set up in the same way as a regular 'agricultural' field trial. Three stones, each weighing about 1½kg, were collected from the beach; the first was hammered on the central male line in the church, and the second on the female side line; the third stone I was very careful not to handle at any time. Each stone was placed in an empty 7lb jam tin, so that it would be shielded from any outside influences. Above each stone was placed a 2-inch plastic flower pot containing Levington seed compost. The pot was supported on wires so that its rim was just level with the rim of the tin. Each pot was sown with seven mustard seeds. Before placing in the tin, the pot was watered by dipping it into water nearly up to its rim, and holding it there until the water showed on the surface of the compost. After draining, this gave enough moisture for the seeds to germinate and grow to about 5cm in height. The three tins were placed in my sun-room to await development. After about seven to twelve days the seedlings were large enough to weight, so they were carefully removed from the compost, washed, blotted dry, and the produce of each was was weighed to the nearest 10 milligrammes.

Germination was somewhat uneven, so I divided the total weight by the number of seedlings, thus obtaining the mean weight of the seedlings in each pot. The reader can imagine my surprise when I found that the seedlings grown over the male stone weighed only 56 per cent of those grown on the uncharged stone, while those grown on the female stone were 69 per cent. I at once thought that this must be due to pure chance; so I repeated the trial twice more, obtaining very similar results. I was still not satisfied, since the differences might be due to some peculiarity of the uncharged stone or the tin it was in. I therefore changed the tins for three new ones and obtained three new stones from the beach. I again repeated the trial, but with the same results. The differences could not have been due to any treatment I had given the plants, because each pot received the same quantity of water and the positions were moved round each day.

I thus had four replicates of the three treatments, i.e. male, female, uncharged stone, so I could apply an Analysis of Variance to my results. This showed that the mean weight of the seedlings grown over the male-charged stones was 27.5 per cent less than those on the uncharged stones, while those grown on the female stones were on average 31.5 per cent less. There did not appear to be any significant difference in the germination between the three treatments as they averaged just over six seedlings per pot in each batch. The Analysis showed that the seedlings grown on the charged stones differed in weight from those grown over the uncharged stones at a probability level of 0.05.

My next step was to see if an increase in charge caused any corresponding increase in damage to the mustard seedlings. This time four tins were set up with stones of various charges from 0 to 167 petrons. Mustard seedlings were then grown in them in the same way as above, and were weighed after eleven days growth. The mean seedling weights were then plotted against the charge of the stone they were grown over (Figure 13); this showed that the weight of the seedling was inversely proportional to the charge of the stone. However, this did not prove that the cause of the decrease was the charge, since it might have been due to the power of the stones, i.e. the product of the charge multiplied by the weight. To test this I

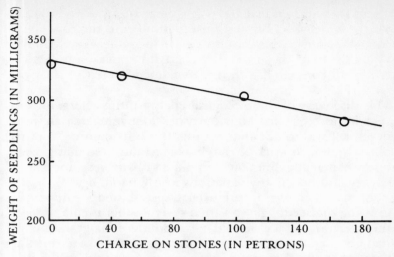

Figure 13. Effect of increasing charge on weight of mustard seedlings.

charged four stones together, so that the charge on each was the same, although their weights varied from about 200g to 1.6kg. Seedling weights, when they were grown over these stones, showed very little difference, thus proving that the factor concerned was the charge on the stones and not their power.

This meant that I could use the decrease in weight of the mustard seedlings as a means of assessing the vital charge in the stones. This was extremely useful, since it provided a means of substantiating any assertions I might make as a result of dowsing by means of a completely objective technique. The snag was that this could take up to ten days to complete, as compared with a matter of minutes when using the pendulum. As I pointed out in Chapter 3, the idea of using living material to estimate the effects of a treatment given to it is certainly not new in principle, and is known as bioassay. As will be seen from experiments described later in this chapter, care has to be taken to ensure that when comparing the degree of effects of the treatment with that of another, they must be comparable; thus it is not possible to compare quantitatively the effects of Bluestone with those of a male charged stone, or indeed two tests done at different times.

If the male and female charges had this effect of reducing

the growth of mustard seedlings, what about the additional
charge which I had found on Bluestone and the dolerite? I
tried these out on the mustard seed in the same way and found
that this time the size of the seedlings was significantly
increased compared with the uncharged stone.

This discovery of the biological effects of this energy was of
such importance that I obviously had to investigate it in some
depth if I was to obtain any insight into its nature. The first
objective was to work out a reliable technique so that I could
be sure than any differences in plant growth were due to this
energy and not to any variations in my handling.

As noted above I had used a peat-based compost for
growing the seedlings, so I tried several other media to see if
they were any better. Several correspondents had asked why I
had not used the standard method of germination testing, i.e.
growing the seed on damp filter paper. I tried this and found
the root hairs penetrated the paper, so that the roots were
damaged when removing the plants from the paper for
weighing. I also tried several other growing media, such as a
soil-based compost (John Innes No I), sand, and vermiculite.
The first two of these were useless because the quartz grains in
the sand acted an an interrupter, so that I got no significant
differences in growth. The vermiculite was better, but suffered
from the same difficulty as filter paper, in that I could not
easily separate it from the roots. I therefore reverted to the
soilless Levington peat compost, but this time using their
'Combined Sowing and Potting Compost' which contains
some fertilizer. Another modification was that I increased the
number of seeds to twelve (or even twenty if the seeds were
very small). This then became my standard technique,
although other means were devized later when I had to
investigate special problems, for example if the differences in
growth were expected to be small, when I used three two-inch
pots in each tin (see Plate 9). This saved considerable time
compared with my original experiment where I had to repeat
the test a number of times.

    If there were three treatments involved, I would then have
nine replicates in all and this allowed statistical analysis. Over
a very large series of such experiments, repeated three times
or using three pots, I found that a difference in weight of as
little as 6 per cent from the untreated seed would be significant

Table 1: The effect of charged stones on growth of various plants

Percentage difference in growth from untreated plants

Crop	Male Charged	Bluestone	Black Line
Wheat	−13.1	+14.6	
Barley	−9.9	+30.0	+16.7
Oats	−21.0	+42.8	+19.2
Grass	0		
Mustard	−14.8	+42.9	+22.9
Kale	−18.3	+12.0	+29.8
Rape	−15.1	+11.4	+20.2
Parsley	−23.5		
Celery	−26.1		
Carrot	−28.2		
Peas	−26.4	+43.5	
Broad Beans	−5.2	+34.8	+17.2
Sweet Peas	−22.1	+51.1	+4.0
Mung Beans	−7.3	+8.4	+5.5
Beet	0		
Lettuce	0	+48.0	
Cress	−21.5	+62.5	

at a probability of 1 in 100, and that usually the difference found in the treated seed was at least twice this figure.

So far I had been working only with mustard seed, and it was clear that I would have to see if other species of plant reacted in the same way. The number of plant species which might be tested was obviously legion, so I selected two or three species from each of the main botanical families, e.g. Cereals, Legumes, Umbelliferae, Cruciferae, and so on. The species selected were mostly vegetables which I was already growing in the garden, together with a few field crops of which I was able to obtain seed. These were all tested in exactly the same manner I had used with the mustard seed, and the results are shown in Table 1. The figures are expressed as percentages of the mean weights of the untreated plants. I could well have included more species if the process had not taken so long (some species took two or three weeks to germinate, and also I could not test more than one species at a time on all four types of stone or the magnet, together with the uncharged stone for comparison, so the whole series took me about three seasons to complete). If there had appeared to be any very marked difference between species, it might have been worth continuing further. Only beetroot and lettuce appeared to be unaffected by the male charge, but, together with grass, these were difficult to examine and I probably simply failed to detect the differences in growth. Maby and Franklin [31] particularly noted the effect of their underground streams on Sweet Pea and Parsley, and this also showed up in my own experiments. The differences in figures for the various species are also very noticeable, but I consider that this might well be due to the very different times between sowing and harvesting, since the growth rate was very different in the various species.

It was not clear from this whether the growth rate of the plants grown over the variously charged stones was permanently reduced, or increased, as compared with the untreated plants, or whether they tended to recover. To investigate this, I decided it would be necessary to examine the plants each day. Since it was obvious that they could not be repeatedly lifted and weighed as I had done in the experiments described above, I therefore decided to measure the height of each individual plant each day.

To do this I filled two 5cm 'half' pots with the usual compost. These just fitted into the top of the jam tins containing the charged and uncharged stones. On the surface of the compost was placed a plastic lid in which sixteen holes, 1cm in diameter, had been punched out (see Plate 9). Into each hole a single seed was planted, and after watering as described above, the pot was set in the tin. Shoots started to appear after about four to six days, and the height of the tips above the plastic lid was then measured with a millimetre scale. Since each hole was numbered, it was possible to record the growth rate of each individual plant. This was continued daily until it was clear that the growth rate of the treated plants was similar to that of the untreated ones.

I decided that this rather laborious work should be restricted to only two groups of plants, namely the Cereals (Wheat, Barley and Oats) and the Brassicae (Kale, Mustard and Rape). The results obtained are plotted in Figure 14a for the

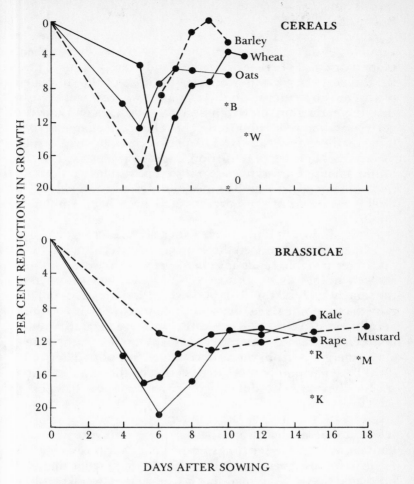

Figure 14. Progressive effects of various seedlings when grown over a male charged stone (*by weight).

cereals and 14b for the Brassicae, the mean height of the sixteen treated plants being recorded as percentages of those found in the untreated ones. It will be seen that the maximum difference was about five to six days after sowing. After this the plants growing over the charged stones recovered rapidly, but they never entirely caught up with those over the untreated stone, remaining about 4 per cent smaller in the case of the cereals and as much as 12 per cent in the case of the Brassicae.

When it was decided that the measurements of the height should be discontinued, the plants were lifted, washed, blotted dry, and weighed, as in the standard technique. These weights, expressed as percentages of those of the untreated plants, are also entered on these graphs, where it will be seen that the reduction in weight was always greater than the corresponding reduction in height. The male charged stone used in these tests was of 120 petrons. As I have already shown, the amount of reduction in growth depends directly on the charge on the stone, so different results would have been obtained had I used stones of different charge, but, no doubt, the form of the curves would have been similar to these.

I had, however, only been using a male charged stone which, as shown, reduced the growth of the seedlings. As was illustrated in Table 1, plants grown over a sample of Bluestone showed an increase in growth, so this had to be examined in the same way. I did this with both wheat and mustard, but the growth of the wheat seedlings was inconclusive owing to poor germination. With the mustard, the greatest difference between the treated and untreated seedlings was immediately after emergence from the surface of the compost. Thereafter the difference rapidly decreased, so that by the ninth day after sowing there was no difference between the two batches of seedlings.

It was not at all clear from these experiments just what was happening to these seedlings, grown over variously charged stones, to cause them to be either larger or smaller than the untreated seed. Germination of seed generally takes place when it comes into contact with water in the presence of oxygen; (if the oxygen is removed from the air, the seed will not germinate in the remaining nitrogen). Enzyme action is then started and germination takes place. Nothing else, other than warmth, is required, as is demonstrated by the germination of seedlings on damp blotting-paper. It is most difficult to conceive that the 'rays' from these charged stones could possibly upset these simple conditions and inhibit the germination, although in a series of most sophisticated experiments Sister Justa Smith [45] found that emanations from a healer's hands did in fact increase enzyme action. Certainly, atomic radiation of various wavelengths can destroy the viability of dormant seeds, probably by damaging the enzymes; but surely the radiation from these stones cannot be of such power? The conditions for growth are far more sensitive to the correct environment than are those for germination, and many things can go wrong to inhibit maximum increase in size.

Most other comparable work has been designed to discover how the 'laying-on of hands' by a healer can affect plants and animals. Dr Bernard Grad [20] in an extensive series of experiments with the healer Estabany, found that barley and other seeds grew into larger plants if the seed was first handled by the healer. He did find, however, that this only happened if the vigour of the seed had first been reduced by soaking in 1 per cent saline solution and then drying in an oven at 38-40°C. He also found that these increases occurred if the healer held a flask of water in his hands and then used this to water the plants.

Dr Robert N. Miller [33] worked with the healer Mrs Olga Worrall, and found that if she held her hands a few centimetres over ryegrass plants, their subsequent growth was increased compared with untreated plants. He also found that water in a beaker that had been held by Mrs Worrell was just as effective in increasing the speed of germination of the ryegrass. He suspected that this action was due to a reduction in the surface tension of the water and went on to confirm that the water held in the healer's hands did indeed have a surface tension reduced by about 10 per cent. He was able to compare this with the action of a magnet with a field strength of 1500 gauss and found that it had much the same effect as the healer's hands in increasing the speed of germination of ryegrass seed.

If I was to investigate any further this action of charged stones on plant growth, be it an increase or decrease, I would have to devise some new technique where I could check the growth at frequent intervals. I decided, therefore, to try some experiments with Mung beans. These are the ones generally used to produce 'Chinese beansprouts', and have the great advantage that they will grow rapidly on the addition of water alone. They have to be kept in relatively warm conditions, and the water changed daily.

In the first of these experiments, twenty-four beans (which together weighed just about 1g) were placed in plastic pots, which were fitted with perforated lids, and a little tap-water was added. (I should note here that our tap-water is quite untreated with chemicals. I once heard an eminent fresh-water biologist exclaim at the almost complete lack of life in our streams: 'But,' she said, 'the water is practically distilled.') These pots were placed in the jam tins in the usual way, the tins containing a male-charged stone, Bluestone, dolerite, a magnet, and an uncharged stone. All were placed in a warm cupboard, and each day for five days the sprouting beans were removed, blotted dry, weighed, and then returned to their pots with a little fresh water. This experiment showed that as from the first day, the beansprouts over the male-charged stone were smaller than those grown over the uncharged stone, but those grown over the Bluestone and dolerite were larger by 5-8 per cent. Those beans grown over the magnet were virtually the same as the ones from the uncharged stone.

This experiment did not, however, make it clear whether it was some radiation from the charged stones which was affecting the growth of the beans, or whether it was some action they were having on the water. A second experiment was therefore planned in which the beans in their plastic pots were kept separate from the stones, and the water used to dampen them each day was kept in glass jars which were placed over the stones. After five days the bean shoots were weighed in the usual manner and it was found that those wetted with water from the Bluestone and dolerite, as well as that from the magnet, were larger, but those moistened with water from the male charged stone were no different from those with water from the untreated stone.

What these two experiments suggest is that the Bluestone, the dolerite and the magnet were having some effect on the water, and that this was possibly due to a reduction in the surface tension of the water which allowed it to wet the seed coat and initiate germination more rapidly. This was evidently not the case with the male charged stone and the action of this must be due to some direct radiation from the stone effecting the germination.

I therefore thought it would be a good idea to check what effect, if any, these stones were having on the surface tension of the water which stood over them, but was not, of course, in direct contact. Miller [33] had used a Du Nouy type Tensiometer with a platinum-iridium ring. The surface tension is measured in dynes per centimetre, by finding the force required to lift such a ring from the surface of the water. I was lucky in having available a delicate torsion balance which I had made many years ago for weighing individual insects, but I had no platinum-iridium ring, so I used a stainless-steel washer instead. After much trial and error, I managed to devise a technique with this set-up so that I could get repeatable figures from the various samples of water. My final conclusions were that the male-charged stone increased the surface tension by about 5 per cent compared with the untreated tap-water. The Bluestone and dolerite, however, decreased it by about 2-3 per cent. The magnet, on the other hand, at first decreased the surface tension by about 4 per cent and then increased it by as much as 3 per cent. This ties up well with Miller's finding that the energy transfered from a ceramic magnet placed in the water, was dissipated after about twenty-four hours. These experiments do seem to support the idea that the effect found on plants by the Bluestone and dolerite is due to a small inherent magnetic charge in them. The evidence from the study of the surface tension of the water kept over the male-charged stone would suggest that, as the surface tension was apparently raised, a delaying effect occurred on the germination. This was borne out in the first experiment where the beans were grown directly over the charged stone. However, when they were grown away from the charged stone in the second experiment and only charged water added, although its surface tension had been raised by about 5 per cent, the weight of the bean shoots was no different from those grown with untreated water. There must therefore be some radiation coming directly from the stone to the seeds to have such an effect.

I think we can now summarize the main points which we have discovered about the effects of these charged stones on plants. Firstly, both male- and female-charged stones slowed down the growth of most plants and this reduction was proportional to the charge on the stones and not to their power. This meant that I could now use the growth of plants, in particular mustard seedlings, to assess objectively any findings which might be suggested by my dowsing. Both

Bluestone and dolerite, on the other hand, increased the growth of the seedlings, this action taking place from the initiation of germination. This effect seemed to be very similar to that of a magnet, and was probably due to a reduction in the surface tension of the water used to moisten the seeds. The action of the male-charged stone on the seeds was rather slower and did not appear to be similar to that of the magnet.

It was pointed out by some unkind sceptics that the whole of these results from experiments with plants might well be due to my wishful thinking which was influencing the plants to grow as I wanted. This is generally known as the 'Backster Effect', after the recent describer of this phenomenon, although it was known to some extent as early as 1904 and described by Sir Jagadis C. Bose in 1922.[6] Cleve Backster,[2] a polygraph expert, one day connected his 'lie detector' to the leaves of a Philodendron plant and found that it reacted violently to a 'threat-to-well-being' such as his *thought* of burning a leaf with a match. He later found that the plant reacted to the timed death of brine shrimps and to his thoughts when he was many miles away. The Revd Franklin Loehr [28] had also found that prayer was an effective means of increasing the growth of plants. I had, therefore, to check that my thoughts were not causing the differences in seedling growth which I had been recording.

I designed two experiments, the first which was a 'double-blind' with the help of my wife. Three identical tins were labelled A, E and G, and in my absence my wife placed in these the Bluestone, a male-charged stone, and an uncharged one, and covered the stones with a disc of card, so that I could not see which was which. In the meantime, I had sown three pots, labelled X, Y and Z, with twelve mustard seeds and by a process of random selection, one of these were placed in each tin. When they were sufficiently grown, I removed the pots and weighed them in the usual manner. Only then did we remove the cards from the tins and discover which stone was in which tin. What I found was that the seedlings grown over the Bluestone were some 15 per cent heavier, and those from the male-charged stone 8 per cent lighter, than those grown over the uncharged stone, in spite of my being quite ignorant of the charges during the period of growth and when I weighed them.

The second experiment was the opposite way round and was designed to check the findings of Revd Loehr. [28] This time I placed three uncharged stones, straight from the beach, in tins now marked +, 0 and -. To detect even a small difference, this time I put twelve seeds in each of the three tins. Each morning, when I rotated the position of the tins, I concentrated on the one marked +, telling the seeds to grow rapidly, and the ones in the tin marked - I told not to grow at all, or at best slowly. I completely disregarded the tin marked 0. After five days the seedlings were large enough to weigh, and I then found that there was no significant difference between the seedlings in any of the three tins. In actual fact those in the + tin were slightly smaller, and those in the - tin slightly larger, than those in the 0 tin! It seemed therefore clear that my thoughts were not as effective as Revd Loehr's prayers, and were certainly not producing any results which I might be anticipating.

As the reader will have noticed, all the experiments described in this chapter were carried out using plants. It would be most instructive to discover whether these charges on stones have any similar effect on animals and therefore whether ley energy might affect human beings. Grad [20] did carry out experiments with mice, and found that the healing of wounds was accelerated if Estabany held his hands over the cages twice a day. I have not myself tried any experiments on animals with my charged stones because I have not really got suitable facilities for such work. Such experiments are not, however, beyond the scope of an average sixth-form school biology laboratory, if they used insect populations such as fruit-fly (*Drosophila*) or meal-worm (*Tenebrium*). Most text-books on practical biology give full details for studying population growth of these insects under controlled conditions. Batches could be set up over charged and uncharged stones, as has been described in this chapter, and any results obtained would constitute entirely original research, which would be worthy of publication.

I have described these experiments with plants in some detail for a number of reasons. Firstly, I think that it is an important illustration of the influence this form of energy, locked in stones but flowing between them, has on something other than the dowser. In fact, these experiments could be carried out entirely without any skill in this art, and I think it is important that they should be repeated by other investigators with seedlings of a much wider range of species, in order that some clue can be obtained of the diversity of effects and the possible reasons for them. This will probably entail the investigation of the whole phenomenon of interrupters.

Secondly, it is perfectly possible to measure the size of a charge of a stone or the strength of a line simply by weighing the seedlings grown on and off it. As a technique for obtaining such measurements, this has its limitations in practice. Compared with the use of the pendulum and gyrometer, which only takes a few minutes to complete, a bioassay may take up to fourteen days if the seedlings are slow to germinate and grow sufficiently large to weigh accurately. Also, as was shown in Figure 14, the depression in growth is not directly related to time and it is only possible therefore to compare pots of seedlings grown at the same time and under similar conditions.

Thirdly, these studies would seem to indicate that the energy flowing along ley lines is not always beneficial and in laying down this system of lines megalithic man may have been trying to rid the area of an undesirable form of energy. The ancient Chinese geomancers were apparently well aware of this dangerous aspect, as described by Eitel [12] and were horrified when ignorant Europeans built their houses on a 'Dragon Line'. This idea might also lead to a re-interpretation of the dream I described in Chapter 4. Is it possible that the people I saw surrounding the stone were trying to 'degauss' the stone of its undesirable energy? The fact that they appeared to be passing something round in an anti-clockwise (widdershins) direction might well support this.

7
More of Lines and Interrupters

Now that I had a truly objective method of measuring these energy lines I had observed running between the charged stones, it was possible to examine in more detail the way in which this energy behaved. Since this energy appeared to be indistinguishable from that which I had found flowing along true ley lines, a study of it might give me a better understanding of this mysterious phenomenon. For example, is it possible that megalithic man, or whoever set up these ley lines, had charged stones and other objects and placed them in straight lines so that the energy flowing between any two stones carried on to others in the same line? If this is true, it must be shown that there is then a greater flow of energy than when they are not so aligned.

To investigate this, I set up two stones (Nos 12 and 21), both of fairly high power, on the church gallery, screened at both ends. A third stone (No 7), of lesser power, was then placed 20 feet beyond stone 21, but 3 feet from the line extended from that between 12 and 21. As will be seen from Figure 15, this

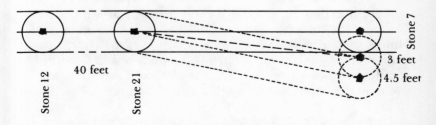

Figure 15. Effect of moving a stone 3 feet and 4½ feet out of line with two other stones.

just allowed the parallels of the line between 7 and 21 to overlap those on the original line extended from stones 12 and 21. The strength of the line between stones 7 and 21 was then measured with the gyrometer and found to be 148.8 petrons. Stone 7 was now moved to a position 4½ feet from the centre of the direct line between stones 12 and 21, and the strength again measured. (Care had to be taken that the gyrometer was still inside the parallels of the line between 21 and 7, i.e. some 8 feet from stone 21; beyond this point there was no detectable line running on because of the screen at the end of the gallery.) The strength of the side line was now only 111.5 petrons, a reduction of just over 25 per cent, due to the three stones not now being in a straight line. My conclusion from this was that, if three stones lie sufficiently near to a straight line so that their parallels overlap, conditions as outlined in the equation given in Appendix B (2) become effective and energy is passed from one sector of the line to another. If, however, the parallels do not overlap, the separate sections of line are similar to discrete energy lines running through the stones and have less direct effect on each other. There is, therefore, a distinct gain in strength of a line if its various sections are, at least, approximately in a straight line.

All this was, of course, determined by using the pendulum as a means of measuring the effect of moving these stones. It was, however, possible to check this conclusion by growing mustard seed both on and off the line, and it was thus found that the information obtained by dowsing could be confirmed objectively.

In view of the possible application of this conclusion to ley lines, it is of interest to consider just how approximate to straightness this line must be to avoid losing strength. It is obvious that the further apart stones are, the closer to a straight line they have to be if their parallels are to overlap. Indeed it, is possible to calculate that if three stones, each almost zero in diameter, are 1km apart, they may not depart from the straight by more than 0.08 seconds of arc. Obviously standing stones are always larger than this; if, say, they are 1 metre in diameter, the divergence could then be 0.14 seconds of arc.

If this rule of straightness is so strict, what about stone circles, where many observers have noted the flow of energy round the stones? The constructors of Stonehenge may well have known about this situation and overcome it by joining the upright stones by a series of lintels, thus connecting adjoining stones and in effect making the entire structure into a single stone. On the other hand, the stones of a stone circle may be so close that they are almost touching, and there would then be a large overlap in their parallels. If there are sufficient stones making up a circle, their parallels may still overlap sufficiently, and a free flow of energy will flow round the circle. The Thoms[46] give a list (their Table 311) of some eleven circles that they believe were still relatively complete, together with their diameter and number of stones. These circles varied from 20.9 to 106.2 feet in diameter, with a mean of 68.4 feet. From the data I gave above, it is possible to calculate the minimum number of stones making up a circle of given diameter so that their parallels will still overlap. Assuming the stones average 1m in diameter, some 12.9 stones would be required for a circle 68.4 feet in diameter. In actual fact, the mean number of stones in the Thoms' table is 13.5. However, on inspection of their data, three of their eleven sites would not have had a sufficient number of stones, with one marginal case, if the stones were only 1m in diameter.

I had discovered how to create these energy lines, but as yet I had no means of destroying them. At times I felt rather like the sorcerer's apprentice in that I had set flowing a flood of lines and did not know the spell to stop the flood. In fact, at one time the church became so full of lines from charged stones that I was in grave danger of having to abandon its use for further investigations.

The recipes for reducing the effects of 'noxious' (black) streams and lines are many and wonderful and have occupied much of the dowsing literature in recent years. They have been reviewed by Michael Guest, [22] including details of the methods I used and described in the first edition of this book. These techniques appear to range from the purely psychological to the purely physical, such as those which I myself had investigated. We are, however, only concerned with the techniques which may lead to some enlightenment of the nature of ley lines.

In Chapter 3 I described how sheet-iron or wire-netting of mesh smaller than 35mm could prove an effective screen for

lines I had set up between two charged stones. I investigated
this further by setting up two strips of iron-sheet, each 65mm
in width, on a line between two stones. The gap between the
two strips was gradually closed until the line vanished; at this
point the gap between the strips proved to be 35mm for a male
line and 50mm for a female line. Whether this difference is
connected with the difference in wavelength, described later, I
am not at all sure. I also found that, if the gap between the two
strips was moved away from the central line, the   line
vanished, and that, if a strip 35mm (50mm for female) wide
was placed in the exact centre of the line, it was again broken.
In fact it would appear that if a disc of iron, diameter 35mm
for the male line and 50 for the female, is placed in the exact
centre of the line, it will be broken. My conclusion was, if a line
were to be broken with an iron stake, as is recommended by
many dowsers, it would need, to be really effective, to be at
least 50mm in width and placed on the exact centre of the
line.

What do these experiments indicate about the nature of
these energy lines? I think it is clear that the line running
between two charged stones is very narrow indeed, and, as we
have seen, this line or 'ray' is surrounded by a field equal to
the size of the rate, i.e. to the width of the parallels. If the
central line is blocked, the surrounding field vanishes.

Recently, dowsers have turned to treating the source of the
line, i.e. the stone or other object concerned, if it is accessible.
The generally accepted method of doing this is to place a few
chips of amethyst on the stone, this being considered enough
to 'kill' it. Using some amethyst chips given to me by a stone-
polishing friend, I placed three stones, A, B and C, in line and
measured the strength of the lines between B and C with the
gyrometer. I then placed the amethyst chips on stone B and
found that the strength of the line had been reduced from
117.0 to 63.8 petrons. I then removed stone B and measured
the strength of the line between stones A and C, finding it also
to be 63.8. This proved that I had 'killed' stone B with the
chips, but not the line, which continued straight through it as
if it had not been there. I do not feel the expression 'killing a
stone' is very apt, because the chips do not completely remove
the charge in the stone; it is still there after the chips are
removed. I feel that 'masking' a charge is a more appropriate
term.

If amethyst chips would do this, what other materials are effective? Going through my small collection of geological speciments, I tried these and other materials, to see if they too had this power. I soon found that besides amethyst, quartz crystals, jasper and flint all gave a good masking effect, while dolerite, serpentine, pegmatite and quartzite all gave some masking, but were less effective than the rocks with larger quartz crystals. Neither Lewisian Gneiss, Torridonian Sandstone or glass had any effect, nor did the metals iron or lead, which, as we have seen, can block a line. No other metals (with the exception of aluminium, which I later discovered is an interrupter), that I tried gave any masking effect. It rather looks, therefore, as if the active materials are those which have relatively large quartz crystals in their make-up. The fact that glass appears to be quite inactive is rather interesting. The chemical constituent of quartz is silicon dioxide, while glass is made up of various mixtures of metallic silicates. Glass is, however, amorphous, i.e. not crystalline in structure. If silica is the necessary constituent of these masking materials, it is clear that it has to be present in the form of fairly large crystals. (The connection with the much discussed 'silicon chip' is not lost in that both rely on the presence of free electrons). It would also appear that low grade (i.e. much crazed) quartz crystals are just as effective as the semiprecious stones such as amethyst (and they are, of course, much easier to come by). There is a ready supply of such crystals in the faults of the Lewisian Gneiss in the Shieldaig area, and in subsequent experiments I used this source of material.

I particularly wanted to know what quantity of this material would be required to mask the charge on a standing stone of known weight. What I did was modify the experiment with amethyst, which I described above, but this time using only two stones, adding quartz chips of known weight and measuring the strength of the resulting line. Full details of this work are given in Appendix C, together with an equation giving the weight of quartz required. In short, I found that the larger the standing stone, the less quartz *per kilogramme* was needed to mask its charge. Thus with a stone weighing 1kg, 1.8g of quartz is needed to mask the charge completely, but with a stone of 100kg, only 19.0g is required — not 1.8 x 100 as it would be if directly proportional. It remained to try this out in the field. As previously described, the Rhu-na-Bidh Stone

weighs about 374kg, and from the equation given in
Appendix C, I found that 20.3g of quartz chips should
completely mask it. This stone has a number of lines running
through it, but it also has one line coming from Meall
a'Gharbhgair, which apparently ends here. If the stone were
completely masked, this latter line should vanish, while the
others would only be reduced in strength. I therefore found a
quartz chip weighing about 21g and, having found the exact
whereabouts of this line with the aid of the Oasis Rod, I placed
the chip on the Rhu-na-Bidh Stone. The result was that I could
then find no trace of this line from Meall a'Gharbhgair, and,
on checking the remaining lines round this stone, I found they
were much reduced in strength, since they were now travelling
twice the distance between one stone and the next.

This masking effect of quartz crystals is apparently similar
to Lethbridge's interrupters and seems to work if placed
anywhere within the field surrounding the charged object.
From the equation given in Appendix C, it is clear that this
interrupter needs to be present in sufficient quantity to have a
full masking effect. Whether this is true of other interrupters is
not known, but it is at least clear that much more work is
needed to elucidate the mysterious properties of these
materials.

This Rhu-na-Bidh Stone is an important ley centre and is
less than 100m from my church which, as it is built of dressed
stones, must have received some charge from the masons
cutting the stones used to build it. On surveying the Rhu-na-
Bidh Stone I had, however, noted no lines running towards
this (relatively recently-built) church, whereas there surely
should have been. I thought I had better make sure of this, so I
walked up and down the side of the church nearest the
standing stone with the Oasis Rod in my hands. After much
searching I was just able to detect two weak lines running from
the standing stone towards those parts of the church where I
had noted the two blind springs, as described in Chapter 1. I
carefully located the centres of both these lines and hammered a
small stone on each. On measuring the charges on these two
stones with the gyrometer, I found they were 53.6 and 52.5
petrons, and on measuring the distance between the standing
stone and the two blind springs, I found these figures to be
78.7 and 87.5m.

I have repeatedly mentioned using the line between these

two blind springs in the church to charge stones, and the strength of this line averages about 118 petrons. The combined mass of the dressed stones making up the church must be very considerable, and, if this was their overall charge, these two lines running from the Rhu-na-Bidh Stone should be far stronger than the above figures suggest. There is also the difficulty, which I have mentioned previously, that on throwing stones at the church wall, I could obtain no indication of a charge on the outside of the walls. What, then, was wrong with my theory that an energy line always runs between two charged objects?

It will be recalled that when I was describing my early work in the church, I had been unable to locate any geodetic lines under this building, such as Underwood described, and I had assumed that the modern architects had been unaware that a sacred edifice ought to be sited over a suitable pattern of such lines. I had also found these two blind springs in the church at either end of the central line; but from what Underwood said, this pattern may be no more than a phenomenon which forms at either end of a geodetic line of any kind. I had also found blind springs at most, if not all, ley centres, and since such centres usually have an odd number of lines running to them, one of these lines must terminate there and form a blind spring. Also mark stones, where two lines cross, do not show any indication of such blinds springs. What else was my church lacking which is present at a ley centre and which attracts lines? The answer might be 'crossed streams', but I think there may be another.

As mentioned earlier, the church is built of dressed blocks of sandstone on the outside and rough stone within, the intervening space being filled with miscellaneous rubble. This rubble was undoubtedly collected locally from the surface of the underlying Lewisian Gneiss and must, therefore, contain a fair proportion of quartz and jasper found in the dykes. Any charge collected by the sandstone blocks when they were being dressed would therefore tend to be masked by the quartz in the rubble. This idea supported by the observation that the charge on the church was not completely masked, i.e. there was insufficient quartz in the rubble, as shown by the weak lines I found running to the Rhu-na-Bidh Stone. Also, the charge on the church was still detectable inside the building, and in fact this was of an order that one might expect from a charge on the external stones. What happens when a charge is masked with quartz chips? No charge is detectable outside the stone, but it must still be present within, because it emerges again when the chips are removed. I see no ready means of testing this hypothesis short of removing all the rubble from the inside of the church walls — which, to put it mildly, is hardly practicable.

Recently, Aubrey Burl[9] has studied a certain recumbent stone circle in the foothills of the Grampians. Here he found a large prostrate block set between the two tallest monoliths of the circle. Of particular interest, he noted white quartz chips scattered round the prostrate stone. His interpretation of this was that megalithic man had somehow associated this white quartz with the moon, an hypothesis which would be most difficult to test experimentally.

What is certain, however, is that these quartz chips would have masked any charge on the prostrate stone, but would not interrupt the flow of energy between the two adjoining tall stones, though they might at least reduce its strength. Whithout knowing the precise purpose for which the prostrate stone was intended, it is difficult to suggest why the builders should have wished to mask it, but it seems fairly clear that they must have known what the results of scattering round a quartz interrupter would be.

If charged stones are set out in a circle, it must be concluded from what we have already discovered that lines will run from each stone to every other stone on the circumference. This is obviously rather wasteful of the stored energy and two alternative means of overcoming this are available, both of which appear to have been used by the megalithic builders. One way was to set a charged stone in the centre and thus gather all the power to this one stone (as in my dream, page 73). The other way was to scatter quartz chips inside the circle, but not within the fields of the circumference stones, otherwise they would have been masked; the energy would then be directed round the circumference. Both these conditions have been described by Aubrey Burl [9] from his excavations of existing circles.

To test this idea, I set out on the lawn a circle of nine charged stones (a very common number according to Burl) with a radius of 4m. Nine stones give a circle of rather interesting

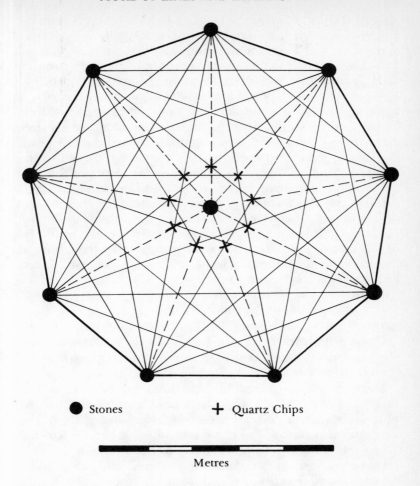

● Stones   ✛ Quartz Chips

Metres

Figure 16. Effect of adding quartz chips and a central stone to a nine-stone circle

geometry (Figure 16). Firstly, it can be set out using only a straight edge and pair of compasses — items much favoured by the early geometers. Secondly, no stone is exactly opposite another on the circumference and, although some thirty-six lines are formed in all, none actually pass through the centre; in fact there is a small circle (1.35m in diameter within such a circle of 4m radius) which is completely free of lines.

In the exact centre of this circle I set a single stone, the

charge of which I had already determined to be 138.4 petrons.
I then measured the charge on this stone with the portable
gyrometer and found it was now 155.7, a quite significant
increase. This had obviously been caused by the lines running
directly from the circumference stones (dotted in Figure 16).
The next step was to place a number of quartz chips on these
radial lines. These were placed 1.5m from the central stone
and therefore outside its field and also outside the line-free
circle mentioned above. I then again measured the charge on
the central stone and found that it had now returned to the
original value of 138.4. This would seem to prove that the
quartz chips, at least under these conditions, were inter-
rupting the lines running from the circumference to the
central stone. Of course the remaining lines shown in Figure
16 would still be present, and to interrupt these it would be
necessary to scatter many more chips within the circle, but not
within the fields of the surrounding stones which would then
be masked. The only remaining lines would then be
concentrated round the circumference.

In this experiment the quartz crystals appear to have been
more effective in stopping the flow of the lines than was the
case with the three stones in line. With the circle, however,
there was no stone opposite on the circumference when the
central stone was blocked with the quartz.

Martin Brennan [7] mentions that the mounds in the Boyne
Valley in Ireland were said to have been completely covered
with white quartz chips. In his interesting decoding of the
carvings on the stones of these mounds, he has shown that
they were certainly designed for astronomical purposes —
perhaps exclusively so. Since the stones built into these
mounds were heavily worked with carvings, they would
certainly be charged and inevitably have entered the local ley
complex. The megalithic builders would certainly have been
well aware of this and, if they did not wish to disturb the ley
environment by structures which were sited exclusively for
astronomical reasons, they would have to do something about
it. Their answer was, of course, to give the mounds a complete
capping of quartz chips, thus effectively masking their
influence. There are rumours that these chips are to be
replaced and this will again remove the disrupting effect on
the environment. Whether this has any calming effect on that
troubled land remains to be seen.

Another example of the use of interrupters concerns the carved stone figures on Easter Island, which were so graphically described by Thor Heyerdahl in his book *Aku-aku*. He describes how these figures were cut out of the rocky hillside by hammering with stone axes; they must, therefore, have received a strong charge from the field of the masons during this process, and being of great size, would then have very great power. These figures were then set up in various parts of the island, thus causing a multitude of strong lines running from one to another. Now, the interesting point is that these figures were originally capped with a much smaller stone cylinder, the function of which was not apparent.

Heyerdahl puts forward the theory that these figures were carved and set up by a master race, possibly white, that had migrated from South America. In the course of time the indigenous population rebelled against their masters and destroyed many of these figures, in particular toppling the stone cylinders that had been placed on the figures' heads. Now, if the master race had been aware of the danger of an excess of lines covering the island, they could also have known that the charge they had given these figures during their construction could be nullified by capping with a suitable small stone. Records show that Easter Island was once much more fertile than is now the case and that it supported a large population. The natives would be ignorant of the significance of the stone caps and in destroying them they would have released all these lines of energy, thereby causing a marked decrease in the fertility of the island — that is, of course, if my observations with the mustard seed is of general application. This again supports the rather disturbing speculation that perhaps we are even now in our ignorance destroying the fertility of the British Isles by fracturing the ancient ley lines with our modern civil engineering works.

It was not until I had completed many of these experiments that I thought of testing the charge on mustard seed, which I found to be male. But much more significantly I found that mustard seed is an interrupter. When the seed was placed alongside a male charged stone, the pendulum refused to gyrate, while when alongside a female stone the gyrations reversed. Does this mean that the seedlings of this species are absorbing the energy radiated by the charged stones and in doing so are in some way damaging their potential for growth?

On the other hand, as I have already shown, most plants are affected in the same way, and not all are interrupters.

Many ley hunters have been surprised to note groups of Caledonian Pine *(Pinus sylvestris)* growing on the tops of hills and apparently forming a feature of classic ley lines, whereas these trees could not have been growing in such a position in the time of megalithic man. All living material has either a male or female charge and could consequently attract ley energy; but this species of pine, which gives a female reaction to the pendulum, is, I found, a powerful interrupter and must therefore absorb this form of energy. Why, then, are these trees found growing on ley lines?

Elm *(Ulmus spp.)*, as mentioned by Lethbridge, is also an interrupter, and this leads to a rather intriguing speculation. During the last decade or so, elm trees in the south of England have suffered a tragic decline in numbers. The primary cause of this is, of course, Dutch Elm Disease and its Scolytid Bark Beetle as the vector. The sudden increase of this disease has been attributed by most experts to a strengthening of vigour of the fungus — a likely hypothesis, but one very difficult to prove, since its strength before the attack was not known. Might it be, however, that at about this time there was a great increase in the building of motorways in this area, with the resultant fracturing and displacing of many ley lines? If these lines changed their direction at this time, they might well have affected the vigour of the elm trees growing in positions previously free from this deleterious energy. Some readers of the first edition seem to have misunderstood this suggestion. They appeared to think that I was advocating that it was the ley energy which was killing these elm trees and not the dreaded Dutch Elm Disease. All I am suggesting is that the change in vigour may have been in the trees rather than the disease which was then able to attack and kill the trees.

8
Black Lines and Wavelengths

During the autumn of 1983, my wife and I had visited the USA, staying mainly in the New England area. While there, I made some enquiries about the very thriving School of American Dowsers in Vermont. I found that one of the aspects they specialize in is the detection and elimination of 'Black Streams', or Black Lines if they are above ground, believing them to be particularly deleterious to human health when running through a house and crossing under an occupant's bed. I well knew that a dowsable line passed diagonally through my own home in Scotland, since I had frequently used it to demonstrate the art of dowsing to interested visitors.

On returning home, I decided to test this line with the Mager Circle (see Glossary) and was concerned to find that the pendulum reacted to the colour black and to the rate of 100, which Lethbridge lists for black and death. I thought, therefore, that I had better do something about 'deraying' it. As mentioned previously, many dowsers used amethyst chips for such work, but since I had found quartz to be quite effective, I thought I would try that. I found two suitable pieces of quartz weighing about 1½kg each and placed one close to the wall outside the house, exactly on the centre of the line, as indicated by my pendulum; the other piece of quartz I placed on the other side of the house where the line appeared to emerge.

On testing the inside of the house with both the Oasis Rod and the pendulum, I could find no sign of the original line, nor has any visiting dowser since then. However, the line can still be detected running both to and from the house in the old position, and this has been confirmed by growing mustard seed both on and off the line and charging stones on it. So what had I done? So far no dowser has been able to give me a rational explanation.

The effect would appear to be somewhat similar to what happened when I placed quartz chips on the central stone of a line of three in the church. It will be recalled that the charge on the central stone was completely masked, although the line travelled from one end stone to the other, just as if the central one had not been there. But why had the quartz acted like this? I knew that it worked well with the vital male and female charges, but that it did not effect the 50 rate charge in Bluestone and dolerite. In order to throw some light on this problem, I set up a new bioassay experiment with two stones, charged by hammering on the ground outside the house just where I knew the Black Line to be. One tin had, along with the Black charged stone, a piece of quartz of about the same size; the other stone was alone and one tin had no stone. Each had a pot of twelve mustard seeds.

On weighing the resulting seedlings, I was horrified to find those from the Black charged stone alone were about 20 per cent heavier than the controls, but that the seedlings from the charged stone together with the quartz were over 50 per cent heavier. What had I done by putting these quartz stones outside my house? This result was so disturbing that I repeated the test, but with very similar results. The true explanation did not become apparent until much later, when I had measured the wavelengths of these lines.

In view of these findings, I decided I had better see what I had really done inside the house and why no dowser could find the line there now. I therefore placed one pot of mustard seed exactly where I knew the line used to cross the central hall, and another on the same side of the room, but some eight feet away from the position of the line. On measuring the growth some five days later, I found no significant difference between the seedlings from the two pots, but to make sure I repeated this experiment, with similar results.

I now had three types of energy lines: the male and female vital lines, a Black Line with a rate of 100, and the magnetic line which I could detect between the piece of Bluestone and some dolerite with a rate of 50. Looking back at the properties of the energy lines, which I had been able to discover, I wondered whether it would be possible to make some sort of a guess as to their physical nature. Many writers have suggested that this energy is electromagnetic in form. Certainly many of the properties of these lines, as described in earlier chapters, bear a close similarity to those of electricity and magnetism — so much so that I have at been at pains to suggest terms different from those used in electricity in order to avoid confusion. There are, or appear to be, some fundamental differences. For example, the rate of decrease in the strength of a line between two stones as they are moved apart does not conform to the inverse square law, and the lines must therefore be in the form of narrow rays. Also the charge of one stone does not appear to diminish when charging another, as it should do under the law of conservation of energy. On the other hand, as the famous Einstein equation $E = MC^2$ shows, energy is equivalent to mass; thus the exchange of charge between stones may result in a loss of mass to the parent stone rather than energy. Since C (the velocity of light) is extremely large, the loss in mass would be far too minute to detect.

The energy of these lines seems to fit most closely with the mysterious Odic force described by Baron Kurt von Reichenbach,[38] who said that its properties lay somewhere between magnetism and light, both of course, forms of electromagnetic energy.

In reading his account, it seemed to me that what he was describing was really a mixture of phenomena caused by the geomagnetic field and local ionisation, e.g. the luminous field seen above a magnet, neither of which were at all clearly understood then in 1844. The point he made was that this force could be reflected by an ordinary glass mirror. This is also true of the lines studied by the Chinese geomancers, as described by Eitel [12]. I tried this out with both my energy lines between two charged stones, and also with the ley lines running from the Rhu-na-Bidh Stone, and found that it was indeed true. This discovery led me to the idea that it might be possible to estimate the wavelength of these lines by the well-known interference method. I will not confuse the reader who may be unfamiliar with this method with a long explanation; suffice it to say that if a ray travelling out from a source is reflected directly back on itself by means of a mirror or other reflecting surface, the two rays travelling in opposite directions are in exactly opposite phase and thus interfere with each other. On examination of the combined ray, one finds bands of high amplitude alternating with areas where the two

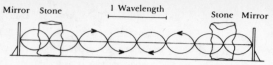

Figure 17. Measuring the wavelength of a line.

rays cancel each other out. The distance between two such peaks (or two troughs) is equal to half the wavelength (see Figure 17).

The two stones were charged in my hand and were laid out 20 feet apart on the church gallery, with screens at either end so that there was a line between, but not beyond, them. A mirror was then set up 20 feet from one of the stones and carefully aligned so that the stones and their reflections were seen to be in line. The area between the mirror and the nearest stone was then examined with the pendulum, and I found that there was now a line here where there had been none before, but that it consisted of bands of strong reaction, alternating with a nil reaction, when the pendulum oscillated instead of gyrating. I found it easier to estimate the position of the nil reaction than those of maximum gyration, and marked off six of these positions on the floor. Measuring the distance between these marks in centimetres gave me a mean half-wavelength of 58.0 ± 0.67, and therefore a full wavelength of 116.0cm. I then repeated this procedure with two stones charged in my wife's hands and obtained a figure of 140cm for the wavelength. From this and the fact that both male and female charges decrease the growth of mustard seed, it would appear that these two charges are really different wavelengths of the same force, and not of different polarity, as some writers have suggested. This is supported by the fact that a stone can be charged with both the male and female rates at one and the same time.

Later I measured the wavelength of a line between the Bluestone and a piece of uncharged true dolerite, i.e. both having a rate of 50, and this gave me a wavelength figure of 90.6 cm. Between two pieces of quartz, with a Lethbridge rate of 36, I obtained a figure of 69.5cm. I also tried this technique out with two stones charged on the ground where I believed the Black Line to be outside the house. This had a rate of 100 to which a pendulum of this length reacted, and the line gave me a wavelength figure of 110cm, which was only a little longer than that for the Bluestone and did not seem right at all.

Just at the same time when I was writing this chapter, an article was published in the *Journal of the British Society of Dowsers* by Sarah Wooster [53] in which she described how the distance between the outer parallels of a dowsable energy line had decreased at the time of an eclipse. Two further eclipses were scheduled to take place soon after this, one of the sun and, two weeks later, one of the moon, so I decided to take the opportunity to check this discovery. The results of my experiments are described in full in an article [19] in the journal, but briefly they confirmed Wooster's observations and added some new ideas.

In these experiments, I had used three lines: the one I had made between two charged stones and used for studying the changes in flow, the Black Line running to my house, and the ley line running from the Rhu-na-Bidh Stone to the Burial Cairn in the village. In making measurements on the latter, I used a plateau on the hill just behind the church, where I found this line was 9.6m above the ground.

The main measurements I made during these eclipses were the distances of both the inner and outer parallels from the central lines, but in addition to this I hammered stones on the central lines at various times. These I used later to measure with the gyrometer the strength of the lines at these times and also any changes in the wavelength. However, on examining these stones at leisure after the eclipses, I found that there was no evidence of any change in the strengths of these lines during these periods.

On the other hand, as had been described by Sarah Wooster, the distance the parallels were out from the central line gradually decreased at the time of the eclipse and then returned to their normal distance after it was over. When I came to estimate the wavelengths between pairs of these stones which I had hammered on the central lines, I found that these had decreased in the same way during the eclipses. I therefore plotted a graph (Figure 18) of these two factors together with the figures I had obtained for the various types of lines described above. From this it was clear that there is a very close relationship between the wavelength of a line and the size of the inner field on either side of the line, what is

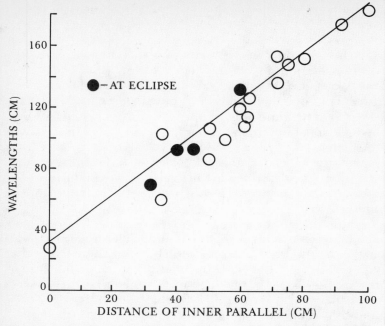

Figure 18. Relationship between wavelength and width between
inner parallels of various energy lines.

known as the 'inner parallel'.

It will be recalled that I was able to show in Chapter One
that the size of the field surrounding a charged object or line
decreases both above and below the object in the form of a
cone or wedge. It follows from this that both above and below
the line the wavelength also decreases. We have seen that this
decrease also takes place at the time of an eclipse, but I could
find no evidence that the line is actually rising above its usual
level at this time, so this decrease in size must be due to other
causes.

This varying field at levels above and below the line and the
accompanying wavelengths provided me with a further set of
points for my graph (Figure 18) and confirmed that they also
fitted this direct relationship; in fact they showed that the
wavelength is about 1.6 times the size of the field (inner
parallel), as measured from the central line. It also provided
an explanation of the curious figure I had at first obtained for
the wavelength of the Black Line. I found that this line was

nearly 7m above the ground where I had measured it at the house wall. This gave it a wavelength here of only 110cm; when I measured it at the true level of the line, I found the wavelength was really just over 180cm.

This graph also shows that when the distance out of the inner parallels is zero (i.e. the line is more than 13.5m above ground level) the wavelength should be just over 30cm. One of the ley lines from the Rhu-na-Bidh Stone runs to the An Fhaire Cairn about 1500 feet above sea level. I calculated the height of this line above the plateau described above and found it to be about 16m; in other words the tip of the wedge below this line was 2.5m above ground level and I could, of course, find no sign of inner parallels. The wavelength at this point worked out at 29.3cm, slightly less than the figure indicated on the graph.

I also measured the wavelength of the line running down the middle of the church, which had always given a reaction on my pendulum to the male rate. This turned out to be rather confusing, because I found that it gave two sets of nil-points, one suggesting a wavelength of 143.2cm (i.e. close to that for the female rate) and the other 62.8cm; in all probability this latter one was for the quartz, of which there is plenty embedded in the church walls. It must be remembered, however, that the main line in the church runs at the level of the eaves, as described in Chapter One.

I also tried this technique on two stones charged on one of the lines running north from the Rhu-na-Bidh Stone. This line also had always given a male reaction to my pendulum, but now produced a wavelength of 184.4cm, very close to that of the Black Line. Are some of these lines in the ley complex therefore Black? Unfortunately when I checked back later to measure the width of the parallels, I found that it had reverted to male, so perhaps it was only a transient phenomenon.

These wavelengths had, of course, all been measured with the aid of the pendulum and the sceptic will no doubt say that they therefore only exist in my imagination. I found, however, that it was quite possible to check these figures by growing mustard seed on the maximum and minimum points of interference, and noting the resulting difference in weight. I did this with the stones my wife had charged in her hands and also the original ones I had wrongly charged on the Black Line, as described earlier, mainly because I did not believe my results.

Three pots of mustard seed were placed where, according to the pendulum measurements, the maximum amplitude of the waves appeared to be, while three other pots were placed half-way between these, where the maximum interference was taking place and the amplitude should be at a minimum. When the plants had grown and were weighed, I found there was nearly 15 per cent difference between the two sets of seedlings.

If these wavelengths are an indication that this energy is electromagnetic in nature, their frequency range would lie roughly between 150 and 500 MHz, and it is of interest to note that radio waves of these frequencies can be reflected by suitable mirrors. Indeed, they fall partially into the band known as Ultra High Frequencies (300 – 3000 MHz). These are, in fact, the frequencies used for radar, which is notable for the fact that it travels as a narrow beam which is readily reflected by suitable materials, just as are the dowsable energy lines. So if this dowsable energy is really of this form, there seems to be no good reason why it should not be detected with a suitably designed radio set.*

This study of wavelengths and the related inner parallels goes a long way to explain the difficulties I was having with the masking of the Black Line, described earlier in this chapter. The mistake I had made was that I was using stones which I had charged on the ground at the position of this line outside the house. When I came to measure the distance of the inner parallels out from the central line, I found that under normal conditions (but not during an eclipse) they were only 73.2cm, instead of 100cm, as would be expected from the rate of 100. This of course indicated that the line was really travelling somewhere overhead. I therefore made a very careful survey of this line and the ground it passed over, and found that it appeared to come from over the Diabaig Hills and then travel across the loch to reach the wall of my house about 7m above ground level. Over this route it was thus falling at an angle of 3° 40' from the horizontal. Having passed through (or round) the house, it reached the beach just below the village road near the old Church of Scotland building. It seems to bounce up again at this point, since it can still be picked up on the main

* See *Postscript*, p.162

road on the far side of the croft land which is even higher than at my house. Since I now had a point where the line was at ground level, I was able to obtain charged stones from the beach and found that a line set up between two of them had a wavelength of 182cm.

The stones which I had been using for testing the mustard and other seeds, as well as the reaction with quartz (page 124), had all been hammered at ground level, usually near the house, and thus had a wavelength of only about 90cm, very close to that of the Bluestone and dolerite line which I had discovered increased plant growth. This is just what I had found when using these stones charged on the ground at the site of the Black Line. Looking back through the records of my past experiments, I found that I had tried growing seedlings of a number of plants over such stones charged on the ground at this point and these had all given an increase in growth, but of just about half the size I had obtained with the Bluestone. Since I now had stones charged on the beach where the Black Line wavelength was at its full size, I was able to repeat these plant tests, but found that there was no appreciable difference from my original figures (Table 1, page 101).

It was clear from this that plant growth is affected not in proportion to the wavelength which, as we have seen, varies with the distance below (or above) the main line. Plant growth seems to be related more to the rate of the particular line concerned. This rate is certainly related to the wavelength, but only at the level of the main line; the wavelength, as demonstrated, decreases both above and below the line, but the rate, indicated by the pendulum, stays constant. Thus the pendulum reacts with the Black Line at the 100cm rate, whatever distance below the line it is used. If this were not so, I would never have discovered this line in the first place.

As I have stated elsewhere, all these experiments were carried out with plants and we now have a fair knowledge of the way this energy works. Whether this also applies to animal growth and well-being I have not as yet been able to investigate, but various observations which have been reported in the literature make this seem very possible.

The main point of the study just described was the discovery that there is a very close relationship between the size of the field round a charged body and the wavelength of an energy line running between two such bodies; both of these change with the height above or below the level of the charged body or line. This change does not, however, occur with the rate indicated by the pendulum, which remains the same whatever level the observation is made; nor, indeed, does the strength of the line vary with the height at which the observation is made. The rate and the wavelength are, however, directly related under normal conditions at the level of the charged body or line, but this relationship does not appear to hold true at the time of an eclipse of the sun or of the moon.

9
Ley Lines Surveyed

We have now spent a great deal of time studying these energy lines which I had found running between charged stones of various types. Although I have, from time to time during the course of this discussion, tried to relate these findings to the true ley lines in the field, it is about time we returned to the study of these and try to apply some of the hard-gained knowledge we have acquired.

In the first edition of this book I described in some detail two local areas where ley lines and charged stones were particularly plentiful, the Shieldaig peninsula and the area on the other side of the loch around Doire-aonar. I pointed out that both these areas were located on the Lewisian Gneiss and were surrounded by the overlying Torridonian Sandstone. I have not so far been able to study the Doire-aonar area in any greater detail but, since I live in Shieldaig, I have been able to survey this peninsula in very considerable depth; the result was that I found many more stones than those recorded in Figure 16 of the first edition, where I plotted only ten stones in this area. As will be seen from Figure 19 I have now found here at least 23 stones and consider that there are probably more on the south-east side around Doire-chlaigionn (the Wood of the skull). This part of the peninsula was probably the most heavily populated in the past, as indicated by the number of 'larachs' and signs of former cultivation. The density of stones here is at its greatest, and I have certainly missed some.

It is only fair to point out that not all these stones would be picked out as obvious standing stones. Few of these stones showed any signs of having been worked, and many of them are just large boulders. These were found by locating the position where lines, which had already been determined,

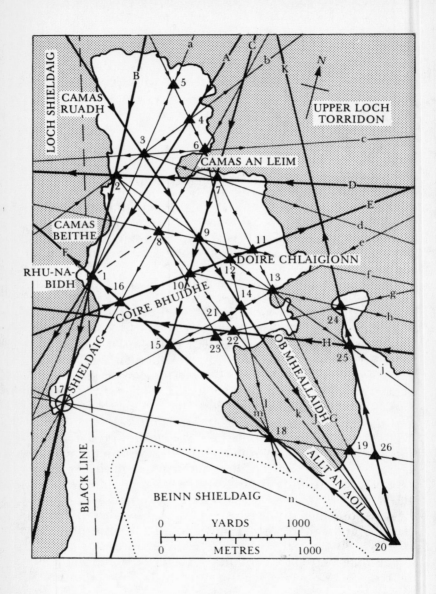

Figure 19. Ley lines found on Shieldaig Peninsula.

crossed. Where in doubt (and it must be admitted that much of the landscape here is littered with boulders of all shapes and sizes, left by the retreating ice) I always checked with the pendulum, using the rate of 50, this being Lethbridge's rate for 'sacred'. Having found such a reaction, I then checked with the Oasis Rod and determined the direction of the lines radiating out from the stone. Sometimes I would check a stone which had all the appearance of a standing stone, being in a prominent position, and which also looked unlikely to be due to deposition by the ice, but only to find that the pendulum gave no reaction.

It will be seen from Figure 19 that, with the exception of just one which appears to run only between two stones (Nos 1 and 8), all the lines are alignments of at least three stones (all sited on this peninsula) and carry on in both directions to other points, many of which have been confirmed, outside this area. These lines can therefore be accepted as true ley lines in the strict Watkinsian sense. The one exception was only recorded very recently; it may well carry on further, but I have not so far been able to discover its extensions.

The total area of this peninsula is a little over three square kilometres and to have this number of stones and lines on it constitutes a very tight complex. I have already shown in Chapter Five that each stone reacts to and is affected by all the other stones immediately around it, so that a change in one will immediately influence all the others. Such a complex is generally known as a 'SPIN' (Segmented, Polycentric, Integrated Network); this is a term which was first used in the Social Sciences and is now used to describe the way in which the network of nerves functions in the human brain. Thus each line is segmented at the stones it passes through, and these make up many (poly) centres; the function of each stone is integrated with the others, and together they form a close network. Although the complex on this peninsula is not entirely separated from the ley centres on the surrounding hills, the very density of the lines here must mean that they act as a single unit.

It will be seen from Figure 19 that these lines seem to converge together on both the south-east and to the south-west; this is because they pass round either side of Ben Shieldaig, following the Gneiss on either side of the Torridonian Sandstone. To the north the lines spread out towards the Gneiss on the Diabaig side of the loch. This, and the many lines in the Doire-aonar area, already mentioned, suggest that the greatest concentrations are over the highly fissured Gneiss, the Torridonian Sandstone of Ben Shieldaig being much less faulted.

Other writers have suggested that standing stones are sited over geological faults and are influenced by the so-called 'Earth Energies'. Thus Tom Graves [21] called them 'needles of stone' and suggested that the stones were so placed to bring up this energy from below and pass it on to other sites as 'overland' lines. Sig Lonegren, [29] when dowsing standing stones, found that the energy travelled horizontally below ground (possibly along a fault line) and then rose to the surface at the site of the stone.

I am particularly lucky in that I have very detailed information on the faults in the Shieldaig area. For many years university geology departments have sent their post-graduate students to this area, with instructions to investigate the local geology in great detail. Over the years we have got to know many of these students and they have been kind enough to supply me with copies of their findings. I therefore plotted a map on the same scale as that of my ley line map, but on a sheet of transparent plastic, with the position of each of the faults and fissures which these students had found. This I placed over the map of stones and lines (Figure 19) and found that in almost every case the stones were over, or very close to, such a subterranean feature.

I have mentioned previously that I usually determine that a stone is indeed a standing stone by the reaction of my pendulum when 50cm long. It happens that Lethbridge also listed this as the rate for heat and it is therefore the rate for such igneous rocks as Bluestone, dolerite, etc. Since Lewisian Gneiss, although not in itself igneous, is a very ancient rock, it is very much contorted with many fissures and faults. Over the millions of years, these fissures have become filled with igneous magma welling up in a hot molten state from below. Indeed, this can be clearly seen in many parts of the Gneiss now on the surface, where the normally grey rock has turned red from the heat of the intruding magma. An example of this is at the position of the fallen stone on Red Stone Hill (Cnoc Ruadh) mentioned in Chapter 2.

To test out this idea that the 50cm reaction of my pendulum

at standing stones was due to the effects of subterranean heat, I tried heating unhandled Gneiss and Sandstone in my domestic fire, leaving them there all night. In the morning I found that both of them gave a strong reaction to the 50cm pendulum, I also tried to transfer this charge to an unheated piece of Sandstone by placing it alongside and hammering, as I had done with the male and female rates of charge. I found that no reaction was transferred, and on testing the heated stone and the hammered one with the growth of mustard seedlings, I was able to check that my dowsing conclusions were correct. It is an accepted geological fact that rocks which are heated, usually by the intrusion of hot magma, have fixed in them the terrestial magnetic field prevailing at the time. This takes place at an average temperature of 580°C, and is known as the 'Curie Point'. It is also interesting that these rocks are often much more strongly magnetized than the prevailing terrestrial field, often as much as 100 times.[26] It seems, therefore, that the 50 rate reaction of the pendulum, which I found at all standing stones, is almost certainly due to the fact that they are situated — or were placed — over geological fissures into which hot molten rock had intruded.

This can be illustrated by two of the power centres included in this survey of the Shieldaig peninsula. I was aware that there should be a stone (No 16 on the map) in Coire Buidhe, situated among the parked caravans there, because three of my lines crossed at this point; these were one from the Rhu-na-Bidh Stone to Stone 20 on the side of Ben Shieldaig, another from Stone 6 north of Camus-an-Leim to the Burial Cairn in the village (Stone 17), and the third from a stone situated above Doire-aonar which crossed the south end of Shieldaig Island (where there may be a stone) to three other stones (Nos 10, 12 and 11) on the other side of the peninsula. All were alignments of at least four stones in this complex, and appeared to cross at this point.

On locating the exact point with my Oasis Rod, I tested it with the pendulum for a male reaction and found that one was present, although I could find no reaction with the pendulum at 50cm. When I examined the geological map I found that the students had been unable to find any indication of a fault in this area. The actual stone is completely embedded in the peat which I think is of some depth at this point, and at times this stone is difficult to locate because it lies under water. It would therefore seem that this is only a 'crossing stone' and not a true standing stone with the necessary 50 rate charge.

The other point of interest lies at the south end of Ob Mheallaidh (Stone 18 on the map) where a number of lines cross. Again I was able to locate the exact point with my Oasis Rod and found that it was located near the middle of the new road from Shieldaig to Annat; this road was built in the late 1960s, and before that there had been only a footpath and stepping stones connecting these two townships. Testing this point with the pendulum showed the male/female reaction of the lines and also the 50 rate reaction which should have been given by a standing stone had one been there. As this point was in the new road (marked by the bollard in Plate 7), it is clear that there probably *was* a stone there and this had been removed when the road was built. Checking on the geologist's map showed that there was indeed a small fault at just this point.

The really interesting fact about this is that the four lines reaching this point passed straight through without being modified in any way, such as direction of flow or termination, as one would expect at a normal standing stone. In fact two of the lines ran straight over the road into the rocky bank at the base of Ben Shieldaig and were there lost. Presumably, had the original stone been present, these two lines would have terminated at this point, since it is clear that the stone was located at this exact point, so that it could collect the energy flowing along these lines and direct it either to Stone 20 on the side of Ben Shieldaig, or to the Burial Cairn (No 17) in the village. The removal of this stone meant that these lines were unchecked so that two of them just 'ran wild' into the rocky side of Ben Shieldaig and their energy wasted. This bears out my earlier remark about the breaking of ley complexes and releasing many 'wild' lines. In this case it is as well that there are no houses on the south side of this road.

We are now beginning to get some idea of what conditions are required for setting up a SPIN of ley lines. Each power centre, be it a standing stone, a cairn, or a stone circle — although I have little experience of this type of ancient monument — must conform to the following three conditions:

1. The centre must be aligned with as many other centres in the complex as possible, in order to conserve and augment the flow of energy;

2. Each centre must be located over a suitable magnetic field, such as that of igneous rock filling a subterranean fissure;
3. The centre must be marked by a suitable stone or cairn, so that it can collect the energy lines and pass them on to other suitable centres in the complex, perhaps in a modified form.

On considering these conditions, it is clear that the setting up of such a complex must have been extremely difficult. There would certainly be some leeway in positioning the stone over a suitable magnetic fault, which would usually be some metres in length, but to ensure that the stone was in line with other stones and also at the point where at least three such lines crossed would be very difficult indeed; in fact it is the kind of task one would now consign to a computer. That such a tight complex as that found on the Shieldaig peninsula could be arrived at by chance seems to be very unlikely indeed. It is fair enough for the statisticians to calculate the odds on so many stones etc. being in line by chance, but to satisfy the other two requirements as well would seem to increase the odds against chance to an astronomically large number.

Discovering the necessary conditions for setting up a ley complex does seem to suggest a possible reason for the use of the Bluestones at Stonehenge. It will be remembered that my original interest lay in why the builders should have gone to such immense trouble of bringing these stones all the way from the Prescelly hills in South Wales. Most archaeological writers seem to be equally ignorant and suggest that it might have been because the builders considered them to be very 'sacred'. Now it is interesting to note that the first reaction of my pendulum over this material (and also to standing stones in general) was to the 'sacred' rate of 50cm. That this was not the real cause of this reaction was not discovered until later, when I found that it was really due to the residual terrestrial magnetism in the Bluestone or in the ground below a standing stone.

On checking the various descriptions of Stonehenge, I discovered that it was situated on a thick bed of chalk, covered by a thin layer of glacial drift. Such a geological formation is not noted for its faults and certainly not for fissures filled with igneous rock. In fact Underwood, [47] in his extremely detailed dowsing survey of Stonehenge, was unable to find the 'crossed streams' he considered essential for such a site. Certainly he found an immense tangle of geodetic lines, but modern opinion is that these were caused by the presence of various stones, and not the reason for their having been placed there.

It is generally held by most astro-archaeologists that the position of Stonehenge was dictated mainly by astronomical considerations and could not have been located anywhere else with the same effectiveness. It appears that the builders were well aware that there should be a concentrated geomagnetic field present at the point where a major stone edifice was to be built. As I have already pointed out, the builders of the almost contemporary Boyne Valley Mounds were also aware of this aspect and overcame their difficulties covering the mounds with quartz chips. At Stonehenge various solutions were attempted.

The first attempt appears to be the so-called Aubrey Holes. These formed a ring of nearly fifty holes, thought by some archaeologists originally to have contained wooden posts, and were part of the first stage of development of Stonehenge. Later these posts were removed and the holes filled in with *burnt* chalk and stones. Here lies the clue to what they were trying to do. Since the infill had been burnt, it would have gained a residual magnetic charge, and in surrounding the site with a ring of such charged material they obviously hoped to compensate for the lack of an underground magnetic field. That this was not entirely successful is clear from the next development of the site.

The builders decided to import, at immense expense of labour, monoliths of Bluestone all the way from the Carn Meini in the Prescelly (Presili) mountains in South Wales. Recently there has been some doubt expressed as to the actual site from which these stones were extracted, since at least some of the monoliths differ in analysis from the stone at Carn Meini.[53] Atkinson,[1] however, says that not all of the Stonehenge Bluestone monoliths are the same, some lacking the spots and others being of rhyolite. Geoffrey of Monmouth, the mediaeval historian, claimed that these stones had come from Ireland, transported thence by the magic of Merlin, while Lethbridge, on the evidence of his pendulum, also maintained that it was from there that they had been brought to Stonehenge. (It is possible, of course, that these Bluestones first went to Ireland from their Welsh place of origin and were then transported back to Stonehenge.)

Bluestone, or prescellite (also known as spotted dolerite), is an igneous rock and usually has a strong magnetic field. The builders of Stonehenge were apparently well aware of this, and since the true Bluestone has these spots of quartz in it, any undesirable male charge picked up while being handled is masked. Moreover, if in sufficient quantity, the Bluestone might be able to mask the charge on other adjoining stones.

If this idea is at all tenable, it must be shown that the Bluestone monoliths at Stonehenge are at least able to mask the charge on the very large sarsens. These, according to Atkinson,[1] weigh up to 50 tonnes, and it is possible therefore to calculate from equation A12 (given in Appendix C) just how much quartz would be required to mask the charge on one of these very large stones. This works out at about 25kg. Owing to the fact that Bluestone only contains quite a small proportion of quartz (the so-called spots) it would obviously be much less efficient as a masking agent than pure quartz. Unfortunately, I had only one piece of Bluestone weighing 410g, so it was not possible to use the technique (described on page 115) in which various sized pieces of quartz were added to charged stones of known weight and the point where the charge was fully masked estimated. What I did, therefore, was to set out a line between two charged, but screened, stones, as in the original technique, and placed my piece of Bluestone on one of them. This apparently eliminated the line by masking this stone, so I added other charged stones until the line reappeared. By adding and taking off small charged stones I was able to estimate roughly the weight of charged stones which would just be masked by this piece of Bluestone, and found it to be just about 7.4kg. From equation A12 I was able to calculate that only 8.7g of quartz would have been needed for this, i.e. it required 47.4 times as much Bluestone as pure quartz. Since we have already seen that to mask a 50 tonne sarsen about 25kg of pure quartz is needed, so we can now say that a Bluestone of about 1.2 tonnes would have a similar effect. The Bluestones at Stonehenge vary somewhat in size, but most of them are estimated to weigh at least this much. They would therefore be effective in masking any charge on the sarsens if properly positioned.

According to Atkinson,[1] the first Bluestones to be set up at

Stonehenge were not dressed to any noticeable degree, and were also placed there some time before the heavily dressed sarsen stones in the so-called Stonehenge III stage. That their effect was not entirely satisfactory is indicated by the fact that these Bluestones were taken down and moved to other positions at least twice, possibly because the builders had not realized that the unspotted and the rhyolite stones were not as effective as the true spotted dolerite forms. This is, in fact, the only rational explanation I have ever seen of why the builders of Stonehenge should have gone to such great trouble to bring in the Bluestone monoliths from such a distance, and it is perhaps rather more objective than the suggestion that they thought these stones were 'very sacred'.

It is of interest to note that no such problems were encountered at the other main astronomical site in Britain, Callanish in the Outer Hebrides. Here, of course, this great monument is sited on Lewisian Gneiss and, as explained above, there would be no lack of a sufficient underground magnetic field.

It must be made quite clear that these faults and fissures in the rock, which were giving a reaction with the pendulum at the 50 rate and indicating the presence of a geomagnetic field, are most unlikely to be dry. They are indeed just the kind of feature through which underground streams will flow, and here is the clue to the 'crossed streams' feature noted by so many dowsers at all ley centres. We have seen how a magnetic field will influence the surface tension of water, and that this in turn will be beneficial to plant growth; this may, therefore, be the origin of the tradition that the water of certain holy wells has curative properties. There is also a tradition that water used to wash the Bluestones at Stonehenge was also beneficial.

After this diversion into a subject of which, it must be admitted, I have no great personal experience, we must return to the consideration of my survey of the SPIN of ley lines and standing stones on the Shieldaig peninsula. It is clear from what has been discovered in previous chapters that these energy lines running between stones cause a reaction of the pendulum at either the 60 or 72.5 rates and that this energy has an effect on most plants, causing a delay in germination. On the other hand, the magnetic field found above a subterranean fissure containing an igneous rock has the opposite effect on plants, causing an acceleration in germination. It seemed desirable, therefore, in conducting this survey of the lines and stones on the Shieldaig peninsula, that I should measure at each power centre:

1. The charge at the 50 rate (i.e. the magnetic field);
2. The overall 60/72.5 charge on the stone (i.e. the combined strength of the lines reaching the centre);
3. The direction of flow of each of these lines (i.e. into or out of the stone).

The overall charge of the lines at the stone and the magnetic field were measured with the easily portable Psionic Scale (see Appendix A(2)). As I pointed out previously, the strength of the lines could be measured by transferring it to a smaller stone and bringing it home to measure on the gyrometer, but this is not possible with the magnetic field. The direction of the flow can be detected with no great difficulty with the standard angle rods used by most dowsers. In using them I find that, as I approach a line and concentrate on the direction of flow, one angle rod flips out in the direction of the flow and back again, across the other road when actually over the line. This is repeated on the other side of the line.

This determination of direction of flow is, of course, a purely subjective dowsing technique, and I do not know of any way, in this instance, of checking the results objectively. However, this method is used very widely by dowsers to check the direction of flow of water in underground streams, and they are then able to confirm their results by drilling a bore hole. It is also used for checking the underground flow of water in a pipe and of electricity in a cable, both of which can be readily confirmed. I think, therefore, that there is no good reason for rejecting these observations of the flow of energy in these lines, even if in this instance they cannot be confirmed objectively.

The results of this survey are recorded in Table 2, except for the directions of flow, which are shown on the map (Figure 19) by arrows on each line between stones. The stones are numbered on the map from 1 to 23 and the lines marked with letters. Only at the Burial Cairn (17) in the village, was it found impossible to obtain a reasonable figure for the magnetic field (50 rate) since, as I have mentioned earlier, it is now buried under the council houses' car park. The male/female charge was there estimated at 40 from the strength of the lines entering and leaving the area, since these are still present. There is no indication, from the change of flow of these lines, that the cairn has ceased to act as a potent power centre.

Table 2: Survey of lines on Shieldaig Peninsula

No.	Name of Stone	Lines in	out	Charges 50	60	
1	Rhu-na-Bidh	4	5	117	84	
2	Camas Beithe	5	2	95	110	
3	Red Rock	5	3	125	105	
4	Badcall High	2	4	138	203	
5	Badcall Low	3	1	138	163	
6	Camas-an-Leim N	4	3	122	170	
7	Camas-an-Leim S	2	6	143	89	
8	Bal-a-Mhinister	3	4	223	122	
9	Doire-Chlaigionn A	3	3	92	113	
10	Doire-Chlaigionn B	2	5	194	85	
11	Doire-Chlaigionn C	2	4	125	64	
12	Doire-Chlaigionn D	1	5	127	127	
13	Ob Mheallaidh N	5	3	138	92	
14	Doire-Chlaigionn E	3	3	108	59	
15	South of Road	4	3	207	50	
16	Coire Bhuidh	3	3	0	115	
17	Burial Cairn	3	6	?	40	E
18	Ob Mheallaidh S	4	4	75	?	
19	Ob Mheallaidh E	1	3	150	72	
20	Allt an Aoil	4	2+	180	50	
21	Doire-Chlaigionn Sa	3	1	139	75	
22	Doire-Chlaigionn Sb	2	4	127	100	
23	Doire-Chlaigionn Sc	2	2	75	133	

On examining Figure 19, it is apparent that nine of the lines go straight through the area without changing their direction of flow. I have drawn these in rather thicker lines on the map and labelled them with capital letters (A to J, omitting I) and have called these Primary Lines because they are clearly more important than the remaining thirteen, which are labelled with lower-case letters (a to n, again with no i). With these latter lines, the direction of flow often changes as the line passes through the stone, or it may even stop (or start) at the stone; these would seem to be of lesser importance, so I have called them Secondary Lines. Most of them pass through at least three stones before terminating, the one exception being that between stones 1 and 8, as has been mentioned.

When considering the Primary Lines, I plotted the male/ female rate charge for each stone consecutively down the flow and noted that in nearly every case the charge started high and gradually decreased as the line crossed the area. Thus line G goes 163, 203, 170, 64, 92, 50, and line B 110, 84, 40. The one exception to this rule is line F which, unlike the others, flows in a north-westerly direction, and is one of the first lines I discovered, as detailed in Chapter Two. It starts at least on the south end of Ben Damph, and possibly even earlier than that, because I have not been able to check it beyond there. It carries on to the Rhu-na-Bidh Stone and over the loch to Fearnmore on the end of the Applecross peninsula, and then out to sea. The value of the charge on the stones it passes through are rather less certain; for example, stone 18 is missing and 16 has no magnetic charge (explained above). Apart from this one line, all the other eight conform to this rule. The values of the magnetic field at the various stones do not seem to show any particular trend; they vary from 257 (probably over-estimated by the use of the Psionic Scale) to 50 and have a mean value of 136.8.

It must be pointed out that these values, and the direction of flow, were all taken during pre-noon hours. Many dowsers have noted that there is a change in the charge on standing stones at the time of dawn and sunset, and Dr Don Robins [40] found that all the electromagnetic and ultrasound activity took place around dawn at the Kingstone of the Rollright Stones, especially at the period of solstice. I thought, therefore, I had better check my records of direction of flow, at least after sunset. This I did at the conveniently placed Rhu-na-Bidh

Stone and found that all the directions of flow that I had marked on the map (Figure 19) were reversed. I may say that I did not immediately decide to repeat the whole survey, this time at night. However, I have checked a few other points, such as the lines around Stone 16, and found that what I had noted at Stone 1 was apparently true of the others.

If it is true that the direction of flow of the ley lines is reversed at both dawn and sunset, what happens about the charge on the stones and lines? It was clear that I had to check this aspect, so I measured both the magnetic field on the Rhuna-Bidh Stone as well as the overall male/female charge about half-an-hour after sunset. The 50 rate charge had not changed appreciably; it was still at about 117, and one would not really expect this to alter if it really is due to the residual magnetism fixed in the igneous rocks below this point. The overall male/female charge of the lines, however, now had a figure of 194, whereas when measured in the day time the figure had only been 84. I really should have repeated the whole of this survey at night, as I suggested, but as this discovery was only made at the time when I was writing this part of this book, I really found it more than I could undertake. However, I did do a few spot checks and found that, at power centres where the male/female charge was relatively low, the charge had increased in value, while, at those at which they were higher, it had decreased. I was therefore fairly satisfied that when the direction of the flow reversed, the strength of the lines also changed.

Examining an intricate problem under field conditions is not always very easy, especially in a complicated situation like a ley SPIN. I therefore decided to isolate the set-up so that I could study it in more detail. I have mentioned on several occasions that I have an area in the garden of fairly level grass, where there are no lines present nor any geomagnetic field from an underground fissure, and that here I could conduct a controlled experiment. I first charged five similar beach stones in my hand, all at the same time, and set these out on the grass, one in the centre and one each about four metres away to be in line with the geomagnetic field as determined with the compass; the other two stones were set out at right-angles to mark the east-west line. Direction of the energy flow in each of these four arms round the centre stone was determined with the angle rods.

What I discovered was not according to expectations and, indeed, most difficult to explain. Firstly, during daylight hours the flow of energy in the north-south line was from south to north; precisely at sunset (and I assume at dawn which was at about 0330 British Summer Time at this time of the year) the flow was reversed, to run north to south during the night. I had made the assumption that the flow was due to solar wind and that it would always be away from the sun. However, as I was doing this near the time of the summer solstice, the sun here sets at about 332° magnetic and is therefore a long way north of the centre of my line, yet the change of direction of the flow in the line certainly takes place at sunset, since I have checked it again at other dates.

The flow in the east-west line is even more difficult to account for. Again, I expected it to flow away from the sun and perhaps change direction at noon, as it certainly did, but the flow in the morning was from west to east and was reversed precisely at noon GMT, i.e. the flow was always towards the sun, and this pattern did not change at the time of the summer solstice.

Before considering the implications of these discoveries, which are included in the next chapter, it is necessary to say something more about the Black Line which I had discovered running through my home. This is marked on the map (Figure 19) as a dotted line running down the left-hand side. After making sure that I had dispersed its influence inside the house, I had done little more about this line, since I did not consider that it was part of the complex of ley lines on the peninsula, which was my main concern. The fact that one of the ley lines running north from the Rhu-na-Bidh Stone had apparently turned 'Black' at the time when I had measured its wavelength showed that Black Lines could in fact form part of the complex, even if only temporarily.

Unfortunately, this Black Line appears to be the only permanent representative of this class of line in this area. There may well be others, but unless they run through a house, one's attention is not drawn to them. Typically, of course, one should have several of these lines, all crossing under one's bed, but luckily we here only seem to have this single representative, so it was easier to deal with. I have discovered that it does not seem to be associated with any of the many standing stones in the area, and there is no fault or fissure marked by the geologists in the Lewisian Gneiss upon which the house stands. Whether it was here before the house was built, or was caused by placing the house in a rather prominent position on the point, is not now possible to decide. If the latter was the case, one would have thought the line would have been attracted by the church which is a much more massive building than the closely associated manse. However, the church seems to have no attraction for it. I have traced it in both directions for some distance, both to the south and on the Diabaig side of the loch to the north, but again it does not seem to be associated with any other feature, either natural or artificial.

I wondered if this line reversed its direction of flow at dawn and sunset, as I had found was the case with the nearby ley lines. On testing this with my angle rods I found that, although I had always considered that it flowed from north to south, both inside and outside the house, this was only true of daylight hours. Half-an-hour after sunset the flow was from south to north on both sides of the house, so it is as well that I had placed a block of quartz on both sides, or the line might well have penetrated the house on reversing the direction of flow, if there had been only one block.

Since this reversal apparently took place, I wondered whether there would also be a change in the charge, as I had found with the ley lines. Since it was not possible to check this directly with the gyrometer, I hammered two stones on the line, one before and one after sunset. The charges on these were checked on the gyrometer later and found to be 93.6 and 116.9 petrons respectively. To further check these figures objectively, mustard plants were grown over each stone, and these were compared with an uncharged stone. This was repeated three times just to make sure of my results, and the mean of each three was taken. It was found that with the daytime-charged stone the growth of the seedlings was reduced to a mean of 90.0 per cent of that for the uncharged stone, but the night-time stone had a mean growth of 117.5 per cent. It is clear, therefore, that if this energy really *is* noxious, it is much more dangerous at night.

Just after I had finished writing the above, I made a trip along the road (B 8056) to Red Point, stopping for a walk on the beach of Opinan. Looking up at the headland to the north, I noted a stone which looked as if it might be of some interest, but on testing it with my pendulum I found it was not charged. However, a few metres to the south-east was a well-cut square stone standing up about 1½m above the sandy soil. Testing this I was astonished to find that the 50cm pendulum revolved *clockwise*, indicating a 'Black' charge; this is the first time I have ever found a Black stone. I had only my pendulum with me, so I could not investigate this stone in great detail, but it was clear that there was a line through it running roughly south. On examining the map when I got home, this stone appeared to be exactly on the extension north of the Black Line through my home, but was just over twelve miles away (nearly forty by road) and ran over some very rough country.

10

Conclusions

The work described in this book started more than ten years ago when I discovered 'dowsable energy lines' running between my charged stones and I decided that if I studied these, I might be able to throw some light on the mystery of ley lines. The assumption had to be made that these energy lines were in fact similar to ley lines. Was this a reasonable assumption? Sir Karl Popper [37] has pointed out that for an hypothesis to be scientifically useful it must be, at least potentially, falsifiable. Would it be possible to falsify this assumption that these two types of lines are identical? Ley lines are, according to the Watkins' definition, alignments of sites, but dowsers, whenever they have studied such alignments, have found that there is energy flowing along them. Admittedly, Sig Lonegren [30] has pointed out that with a few such alignments it is not possible to detect such a flow of energy and he takes the view that such alignments are not really ley lines but are sites which are in line by chance.

Another apparent difference between my dowsable energy lines and ley lines is that this energy can be detected flowing between just a pair of charged stones, whereas ley lines must consist of at least three sites in line to form an alignment. (The criteria of five sites in 25 miles is merely an extension of this, designed to ensure that an alignment found on a map is less likely to be due to chance.) Logically, the increase in the number of required sites from two to three between the two types of line is merely a difference of degree and not of kind, so there is no reason to reject the hypothesis on this ground.

Throughout this study I have taken great care, when a particular property has been discovered by the study of my charged stones, to check that the findings can also be applied to ley lines and standing stones in the field. In every case I have found that such laboratory conclusions can be equally well applied with similar conditions in the field. In the same way, when an observation was made in the field (e.g. the direction of flow of the energy in ley lines), I was very careful to check the conclusions by setting up a controlled experiment with charged stones, often screened from influences of the environment. I can therefore see no good foundation to an accusation that I have been studying only some artificial energy lines and charged stones which have really nothing to do with true ley lines. The view that ley lines are purely 'alignments of sites which ley hunters believe were surveyed and marked in pre-history' [11] does not appear to be a useful scientific hypothesis, because it allows no conclusions to be drawn from it and is not falsifiable.

Most modern writers have dismissed Watkins' theory that ley lines were ancient tracks used by travellers of various kinds. This can hardly be the full explanation since, as I have shown above, in this particular area the lines frequently travel over the sea. However, I do not think he was entirely wrong, although this cannot be the reason they were set up in the first place. As I have described, ley lines can be detected by a dowser even when he is not actually standing on the line, and also it is generally thought that the art of dowsing was much more common in ancient times than is now the case. Since there were, of course, no signposts or maps in those days, a knowledge of the local lines could have been used rather like an AA itinerary: thus, starting at a given stone, say, the traveller would know that he had to move along a certain line until he reached some other feature; he would then move along another line, and so on until he reached his destination. This method would have the great advantage in that the 'track' could be followed in the dark or in a thick mist.

In making any survey of a ley complex or SPIN, there are a number of factors which should be measured so that one has a full record of their values at each centre at that particular time. As I have pointed out, the magnetic field at each centre must be estimated at the time, although it is not believed that this varies from day to day. The number of lines running in and out of the centre (stone etc.) must be noted, together with their strength and direction of flow. When doing this, as we have seen, it is essential to note the time of day and phase of the moon, since these will have some effect on the values recorded. Furthermore, it is useful to hammer a stone on each of the lines, so that their wavelengths can be measured at leisure in the laboratory.

We have seen that from the very detailed survey I carried out on the Shieldaig peninsula that there are three main conditions for setting up a ley centre:

1. Each centre must be in line with as many other centres as possible, in order to conserve and augment the energy flowing in the lines between them;

2. Each centre must be located over a suitable subterranean magnetic field. (Underwood [48] had noted this feature, in that he found one of his 'Blind Springs' at every energy centre which gave a reaction to 'holy ground', i.e. the pendulum would react to the rate of 50, which is also the reaction given when magnetic rock is present. In the same way, Tom Graves [21] suggested that standing stones were placed by megalithic man over Blind Springs and at these points the 'cosmic charge' of the Earth rose to the surface.)

3. These ley centres must be marked, at the points where the lines cross, by a suitable feature, such as a standing stone, cairn, or indeed any of the other features listed by Watkins. This was to collect and redistribute the energy of the line passing through.

If these conditions are to be accepted, what can we learn about ley lines by looking at the properties of the charged stones and lines which I have been studying? Firstly, it is desirable to check that these Watkins features were set up where there are some signs of a geomagnetic field. I have already shown that these centres on the Shieldaig peninsula are sited over fissures or faults which are likely to contain igneous rock with a residual magnetic charge. This, of course, could be checked with a sufficiently sensitive portable magnetometer. In recent work, Dr Don Robins [40] has described a variety of electromagnetic phenomena in the vicinity of the Rollright Stones. What will *not* produce useful results is to place a portable magnetometer on a ley line: this was demonstrated on television (on BBC2 on 11 February 1986) and on finding no response, they declared there is no evidence for ley lines. This is rather like looking for radio waves with a compass and on failing to record them, declaring that there is no evidence for the existence of 'wireless telegraphy'.

Underwood [48] suggested that Blind Springs were part of the geodetic line complex, i.e. they were formed at the terminus of a line. I thought I might be able to test this by breaking a line with a fine wire-mesh screen. I tried this first on the line running down the centre of the church , but found that the screen did not break the line. I then recalled that this line was not at floor level, being at the height of the eaves, and that I had already found that to break a line, the screen had to be in its exact centre.

As mentioned previously, I had used the line running between the Rhu-na-Bidh Stone and Meall a'Gharbhgair to test the effect of masking the stone. I therefore tried placing the wire-netting on this line and then testing with the Oasis Rod for any indication of the Blind Spring round the stone. I could find no sign of it; so it would appear that this feature was only present when the line terminated at the stone. I have, in fact, already suggested that a Blind Spring may be no more than an interference phenomenon at the terminus of a line. Underwood figures the Blind Springs as a spiral. To test this I carefully followed with the pendulum the lines of the blind spring at the end of the church central line and found that they appeared to be in the form of seven concentric circles. It is not easy to follow these lines, and either Underwood or I may be mistaken. If they *are* in the form of concentric circles, this would seem to support the idea that they are, indeed, interference figures, caused by the waves of the energy lines flowing into the centre and back again, rather than straight on through the centre as a continuing line.

However, in the article by A. V. Jones (mentioned previously [24]), he studied some Blind Springs around a standing stone and within earthworks. In each case he found an anticlockwise flowing spiral. These spirals were, however, distorted by the earthworks and tended to follow the sides of the banks of the ramparts. The interesting part is that when the area was later bulldozed flat, he found that the shape had reverted to an even spiral.

But what about the so-called 'crossed streams' which are also said to be present at all ley centres? When I stopped the line with the wire-netting, as described above, I could find no sign of the crossed streams either; but I am not at all clear what these streams really are. Perhaps they are merely fields which are also formed by the terminating line. These experiments really only provide very subjective evidence, and one really needs something rather more positive as proof; but it does seem rather far-fetched to maintain that by placing a wire-netting screen across an invisible line on the surface, one had banished from existence two underground streams of water. There is no evidence that I know of that substantiates the assertion that these crossed streams are, in fact, streams of water flowing below these sites. Possibly they are no more than lines of force below the ground surface that influence the dowser. This is supported by the contention that it is possible to check or divert Black Streams by driving an iron stake into the ground above the line. Even the most optimistic dowser would not claim, I think, that he had actually diverted or stopped a flow of water. In the same way, when I was describing how I removed the Black Line from within my house with lumps of quartz (page 123), I would certainly not claim that I had stopped an underground stream flowing under the floor, particularly as it appeared again on the other side of the house. It is more probable that I had masked its influence over this area.

All this seems to indicate that these rings round the ley centres are the product of the lines which run into them and are not the natural properties caused by the geomagnetic field which, as we have seen, is an essential ingredient of a ley centre. This conclusion really needed testing under more controlled conditions than are found as observations on natural ley centres. I therefore used the five stone complex which I had set up on my lawn to observe the changes in flow (page 146), except that in the place of the central charged sandstone I used a piece of charged dolerite, since this also gave me the required magnetic field which was not naturally present.

I first checked with the Oasis Rod that all four lines, north, south, east and west, were indeed present. I then tested the central dolerite stone to see if there was any sign of the circles (or spiral) which would indicate the presence of a Blind Spring. I found none, but this was to be expected according to my theory that such a phenomenon is only present when a line terminates at the central stone, whereas here the north-south and east-west lines both passed through the central stone. I then removed the east stone and again checked for the encircling Blind Spring and this time found it present. There were seven rings (or spirals), the outermost having a radius of 2.6m.

The charge on the stones which gives a reaction with the pendulum to the vital (or sex) rates (60 and 72.5) is apparently partly geomagnetic and partly from the vital field of the person charging the stone. This is clearly indicated by the difficulties I got into when trying to devise a reliable method for measuring it. That it was partly due to the varying geomagnetic field was proved by the elimination of the psi-factor when I screened the stones and gyrometer from outside magnetic influences. The remaining charge was that which had been induced by the charger and was probably connected with his personal field.

During the course of these experiments I have discovered a number of properties of this energy which may give some leads as to its real nature. Firstly, it appears to form a field surrounding all living, or once living, material, and is not dissimilar to the electromagnetic fields found by Burr.[10] The fact that these charges can be transferred to stones and that their subsequent decay can be prevented by heat or an electromagnetic field would seem to support the idea that we are here dealing with some form of electromagnetic energy, as also does the fact that the strength of the line between two charged stones decreases as the stones are moved further apart. The rate of this decrease, however, is such that it appears to be a narrow beam of energy and not just an expanding field round the stones. The further evidence that we can produce interference phenomena on these lines indicates a wave formation and from this we can suggest that it has a wavelength of about ½-2m. If, therefore, this energy is electromagnetic in nature, it should not prove too difficult to design some form of electronic device which would detect and measure it with far more accuracy than I have been able to do with the aid of a pendulum and gyrometer. One is left, however, with an uncomfortable feeling that if ley energy *is* electromagnetic in nature, it would surely by now have been detected with one of the immense range of electronic instruments already available to the modern physicist. The fact that it has not is, I am sure due simply to the lack of trying. Dr Don Robins [40] has shown clearly that with suitable apparatus a great deal of activity, both electromagnetic and ultrasonic, can be picked up at a suitable site, e.g. the Rollright Stones. The difficulty, as he has shown, is in obtaining the requisite funding. With the current attitude, particularly on the part of some archaeologists, that ley lines just do not exist, any research worker interested in the subject stands very little chance of obtaining the requisite support for the time and money to be spent on what is considered to be a quite unrewarding subject.

It is clear from what we have seen in the studies described in this book that the charges on ley lines, and to some extent other forms of dowsable energy lines, are made up partly of the vital rates (60 and 72.5) and partly magnetic charges; this is made clear by the fact that these charges vary with the phases of the moon and also, in the long term, with the sunspot cycle. That this latter phenomenon influences the geomagnetic field is well known and is generally thought to be due to what is known as the 'solar wind', a stream of charged particles originating from the solar flares. These particles are diverted to the north and south poles by the earth's magnetic field and are the cause of the spectacular aurora borealis.

The nature of this Solar Wind is very much the subject of current research, especially in the arctic and antarctic regions[43,51] where it reaches the earth's surface in quantity. Accounts of this work have not yet reached the standard textbooks and it is not easy for a non-specialist like myself to obtain full details. It is clear, however, from the observations I have described, that the flow of energy in ley lines and between charged stones is greatly influenced by the position of the sun and moon in relation to the earth's magnetic field.

On the other hand, a rather disturbing idea has been put forward by Wing-Commander C.V. Beadon [3] He suggests that ley lines may be thought-waves which pick up good or bad qualities as they travel through space, i.e. they change wavelength. That such waves do exist is apparent from the effects they can have on such phenomena as psychokinesis and poltergeists. Unfortunately, this hypothesis would appear to be most difficult to test in the field since, if we dismiss the materialistic contention that thinking is nothing but a flow of electrical impulses from one brain cell to another, we are left with little conception as to what 'thought' really is.

Beadon's idea is not, however, quite as revolutionary as it might at first appear. Recent ideas in theoretical physics [4] concerning the implications of the quantum theory and relativity, suggest that both matter and thought are merely explicate erruptions on an implicate sea of energy filling the whole of cosmic space. The properties of 'thought-waves' should, therefore, not be greatly different from those of the electromagnetic fields surrounding all matter. Further, Dom Petitpierre [35] has suggested that it may be possible to eradicate ley lines by a ceremony of exorcism, which is surely a purely mental exercise. This idea may also be a possible explanation of the rates found by Lethbridge for abstract concepts, which must exist only in pure thought.

Shortly before going to press with the first edition, it was pointed out to me that as the human body has a charged field and also mass, according to my findings outlined in this book, one would expect that a line should form between two such bodies. This obviously had to be checked, so I decided to carry out a suitable experiment. Two people (both female) were stationed 7.5m apart, in an area where I found no lines to be present; both were given a stone to hammer in the left hand, so that I could determine their respective charges. Having removed these two stones out of the area, they were then asked to direct their thoughts at each other's minds, and while they were doing this, I checked with the Oasis Rod that there was apparently a line running between them. I then placed an untouched stone on this line, approximately half-way between them, and hammered it. To ensure that my field did not influence this line, I used a hammer with a handle about a metre long.

The two participants were then asked to think of something else or, better still, keep their minds blank, and while they were doing this I again checked with the Oasis Rod, but could now detect no line between them. To substantiate this, I hammered another unhandled stone on the position of the previous line.

The values of the charges on the two stones they had held, together with the participants' weights, gave me a figure for their respective powers and from these I was able to calculate from the equation given in Appendix B(2) the theoretical strength of the line between them. I found that this came to 97.3 petrons. However, on checking the charge on the stone which I had hammered on the line between them when they were directing their thoughts at each other, I obtained a figure of only 79.0 petrons. This difference is significant, though we have no reason to believe that the density of the human body is equivalent to that of a quartz-containing stone, for which the equation was designed. It may well be that the human body is much less efficient in the production of power. What is, however, remarkable is that I could detect with the Oasis Rod no line between them when their minds were directed elsewhere, nor could I detect a charge on the stone hammered on the line at that time.

No doubt the sceptics will say that all this was only recorded by dowsing and that as it was presumably the result I had expected, I could easily have influenced the movement of my pendulum. To substantiate my findings, therefore, I grew a pot of seven mustard seeds on each of the two stones I had hammered on the line, using the technique previously described. Germination was unfortunately rather poor, since the seed I had at that time was over two years old, but the mean weight of the seedlings from the stone hammered when the two participants were directing their thoughts at each other was 73mg, while those from the stone when their minds were directed elsewhere or blank, proved to be 107mg, thus showing a reduction caused by the line between them of 31.8 per cent.

This experiment obviously needs repeating by other workers, with a lot more consideration given to guarding against the interference of external fields; for example, the two participants should really be inside a wire-netting cage, with the experimenter outside so that his field can have no influence on the situation; moreover he should be invisible so that the participants do not direct their attention — and a line — towards him.

If these findings can be substantiated, they are obviously of enormous significance. Not only do they tend to support Beadon's idea, [3] mentioned above, that ley lines may be *thought* lines, but also the idea put forward by many authors that these lines may have been used for communication purposes or may even be of importance in facilitating telepathy. What is interesting is that the line only appeared when the two human minds were directed at each other. Had they reacted in the same way as an inanimate charged stone, lines would have radiated out to all other charged bodies in the immediate vicinity. This observation would imply that in a crowded room one is not inflicted with lines from everyone around, but only from those with whom one is in immediate communication. This may help to explain the well-known 'cocktail party' phenomenon, where one only hears the conversation of one's immediate neighbour in spite of the general buzz all round.

The general findings of this experiment really need confirming by other research workers, since they open up a whole new conception of the ley line problem. Up to the time of preparing the second edition of this book, I have not heard of anyone attempting it, but if it is to be done properly the conditions are perhaps a little difficult to attain.

Since it is clear that the ley complex was, indeed, created by men, whoever they were, and is not just some natural phenomenon, can we suggest some reason why the ley complex was set up?

We have discovered that the energy lines running between charged stones (i.e. those lines on which the pendulum reacts at the vital rates of 60 or 72.5) are inimical to, at least, plant growth, and perhaps to all living matter, although I have not yet been able to demonstrate this latter aspect. On the other hand, the geomagnetic field found at all ley centres is beneficial to living matter and it is in all probability similar in action to the effect of the healer's hands.

Megalithic man built most of his major monuments of stone (with the possible exception of such rare structures as Woodhenge), many of them being of dressed stone, and this is true of most of the larger buildings, such as churches, cathedrals and castles, up to the time of the Reformation when in Tudor times bricks were becoming more plentiful. In fact it was just such monuments which Watkins included in his ley lines. We have seen that the stones of these structures became charged within the fields of the stone-masons with this vital force which appears so deleterious to other living matter. It is generally agreed that megalithic man was far more sensitive to his environment than we are today and apparently he realized that he was 'polluting' the environment with his major stone monuments. He decided, therefore, to set up the ley complex or SPIN to direct the noxious man-generated energy lines to points in the environment where there was a counteracting geomagnetic field. We have seen how at Stonehenge he was unable to do this, and the methods by which he tried to overcome this difficulty. We have also seen from the detailed survey of the Shieldaig peninsula that, where conditions were suitable for such an arrangement, it did in fact reduce the charge of the lines, at least during the day. Luckily most of our buildings today are of brick or concrete which are not charged in the same way. Our greater danger today is of disturbing the complicated system set up in previous ages.

In this book I have given sufficient clues to enable anyone to set up a ley line. Should the reader be tempted to try this out for himself, I would most strongly urge him not to do so. A few summers ago I was surprised to discover a number of small cairns of stones built on many of the hill tops around here, presumably by some holidaymaker. As I had not noticed them previously, I tested them with my pendulum and this showed that these cairns were not charged and therefore no energy lines ran between them or to the surrounding standing stones. Had the builder known how to charge the stones, untold damage would have been done to the local ley complex. As yet we have very little knowledge of the potential power for good or evil of this energy, although there are indications that it can be great. Until such a time as we have this knowledge, it is very undesirable to add to or alter the existing system. All of the many stones which I have charged during these investigations have been stored in a fully screened container or masked with quartz chips. I hope therefore that I have in no way contaminated this ancient environment.

To many this landscape appears natural and little changed since the retreat of the last Ice Age. To the discernible eye, however, it is clear that everywhere there are signs of modifications by megalithic man. Indeed, these remains are far more frequent and widespread than those of the vanished crofting communities whose 'larachs' are restricted to a few rapidly disintegrating walls of croft homesteads and shieling sites.

It was not my intention in undertaking this study to get embroiled in the argument as to who set up these ley complexes. This is not a question which can be settled by scientific enquiry, since it is historical — or probably prehistoric — in nature. Throughout this work I have called the builders 'megalithic man' without any suggestion as to when they carried out this work. Ley hunters by definition (see Glossary) believe that ley lines were set up in prehistoric times, although there is no evidence that Watkins stipulated this, since he included pre-Reformation churches and castles in his list of features.

There is some good evidence that the Celtic Church was well aware of what the ley system was all about; I am not suggesting that it was responsible for setting it up, since there is plenty of archaeological evidence [8] that, where it is possible to date standing stones and circles, they were clearly set up in the Neolithic or early Bronze Age. Looking back over my ley hunting activities in Wester Ross, it is notable that, without exception, all the ruins of old churches and burial grounds were sited on ley centres. This is even true of the now barely-detectable site of the chapel at Bail-a-Mhinister. On the other hand, of the modern churches, including the three in the village of Shieldaig, all of which were built during the last two hundred years, not one is sited on or even near a single ley line. When the old religious sites were chosen, it is clear that someone must have been aware of these lines, even if there is no surviving written evidence for such knowledge. However, what so many critics [52] of the ley system seem to forget is that the absence of written evidence can in no way be considered as conclusive evidence that something does not really exist.

Postscript

Further to what I said on page 49 about detecting this energy with a suitable electronic instrument, just as I was correcting the final proofs of this book, I was visited by a fellow dowser who is also a electrical engineer. With his Cathode Ray Oscilloscope we spent a long weekend studying what energy sites we could find round my home. With the aid of a selection of coils attached to the Oscilloscope, we were able to obtain some very interesting results.

For example, on a line between two hand-charged stones, set some 10m apart, we found an energy level of 48 millivolts at a frequency of 200 kiloHertz. At the Rhu-ne-Bidh Standing Stone above my house, we recorded a field of 13mV at a frequency of 20kHz. We then examined two of the ley lines running south from this stone and found that they both had a frequency of 190kHz; that running to the village burial cairn had an amplitude of 20mV, while that to An Für which is nearly four times the distance away was only 10mV. This difference in strength fits well with that predicted by equation A(9). The Black Line, described on page 123, had a distinctly complex wave-form, the greatest amplitude being about 40mV, also at 200kHz. In the church we examined the Blind Spring at the south end of the central line (see page 29) and found a complex field of 185kHz with an amplitude of 24mV. The most surprising observation was on the female side line running level with the edge of the balcony. This had the enormous amplitude of 5 Volts, at a frequency of about 47Hertz, i.e. rather less than that of the mains electric supply.

These observations show a range of frequencies rather lower than those I had calculated with my dowsing technique (page 126), but it is not clear as yet whether we were recording the carrier wave or the actual message, since all waves were complex. These observations do, however, amply bear out my contention that with a suitably designed instrument, it is perfectly possible to pick up and record these energies which I have been studying by dowsing and other means over the past fifteen years.

Appendix A

1. Measuring the charge with the gyrometer

As stated in the text, I had noticed that the longer the cord (rate) of the pendulum, the larger the radius of gyration seemed to be. I made the assumption that the 'inherent' charge for each material should remain constant, as opposed to the 'induced' charge (such as I had found in sling stones). I therefore selected some thirty different materials, each of which had a specific inherent rate as given by Lethbridge. Fifteen of these materials were minerals, such as silica or calcium, or metals such as iron or copper, while the remaining fifteen were organic substances such as certain plants or types of wood. The rates of these materials covered practically the whole range from 0 to 100cm. I then measured the radius of gyration for each material, taking little over half-an-hour in all, so that there would be no appreciable variation with time. These radii of gyration were then plotted against their respective rates, and I obtained a good straight line relationship, giving a ratio of 0.2828 when the radius was divided by the rate. This process was repeated on another day, and I again obtained a good straight line relationship, but this time the value of the ratio was only 0.1583.

This was a distinct complication, since it would mean that either (a) the charges of the inherent rates were varying from day to day, or (b) my powers as a dowser controlling the pendulum were varying. If it was (a) then it would seem that all the inherent charges were varying in the same way, so I thought it much more likely that it was my dowsing that was at fault. As it turned out later, I was wrong in both these assumptions. What was varying was an additional magnetic charge on the materials, but it took me a very long time before I found this out. In the mean time, I set out to discover if there was any predictable pattern in these variations.

In one of his books on dowsing [27] Lethbridge describes a rate of 22.5cm (9½ inches) that he used to estimate someone's psychic potential by counting the number of revolutions of the pendulum of this length before it returned again to oscillations. I had already tried

To Do

Tues - Feb 5/91

1. Call UPS -- Prep Drum's Pkg
   at Alpha.

2.) Any charges -- Drop Stamps
   / Confirm Paid Last m-

3.) Pay RX? for BX/ - ?
   [RX? @ Alpha]
   Look for other

this on myself, by holding the pendulum over my right toes and had noted that I seldom got the same count when I did this at different times. I therefore decided to see if this measurement had any relationship to the variations I had found in the radius of gyrations when measuring the inherent charge of these materials. One day, therefore, I made one of these 'psi' counts over my toes every hour from 6 a.m. to midnight and, on plotting the resulting figures against time, I obtained a smooth curve (Figure 8a); low at first and rising to a peak about 4 p.m. (GMT), then falling again. Later I managed to obtain a few further counts during the period between midnight and 6 a.m., which suggested that the minimum was about 3 a.m., thus completing the curve. I repeated this exercise on another day, when I again obtained a smooth curve, but this time with much less difference between the peak and the trough. This meant that there was a marked circadian rhythm in my psi count, but there was also some other factor which affected it from day to day.

As a biologist I was well aware that there are many biological rhythms related to the phases of the moon, so I decided to see if this was in any way concerned with the variations in my psi counts. Since the maximum in my circadian rhythm was at 4 p.m., I made psi counts over my toes at this hour every day for 29 days, thus covering all phases of the moon. On plotting these figures I again got a smooth curve with a maximum at full and change phases and a

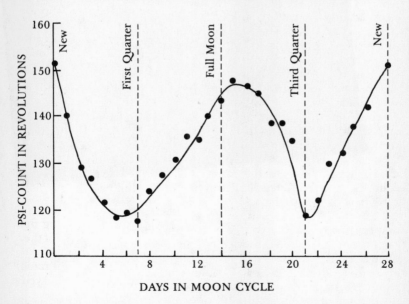

Figure 20. Variations of daily psi count with phases of the moon.

minimum at the first and third quarters (Figure 20). Combining these figures with those of the circadian rythm, I obtained a series of curves, repeated every seven days for the lunar month, with a maximum difference between peaks and trough in the curve for the full and change and the minimum difference in the curve for quarter phases of the moon. All this had taken a long time to work out (about three months in fact) and several hundred counts, but now I had a good psi count for every hour and every day over all phases of the moon. I now had to see if these psi counts were in any way related to the variations in the radius of gyration which I had previously encountered. To do this I used only two materials: zinc, which has the same inherent rate as male, and gold, which has the same rate as female (72.5cm or 28 inches). I had already collected quite a number of measurements of the radius of gyration (S) for these materials, together with the time of day and phase of the moon when they were made. I therefore plotted the ratio (S/R) of the radius of gyration to the rate (since I had already determined that this was constant at any one time for all materials) against my psi count for the time at which the measurements were made. These figures were subjected to an Analysis of Covariance, and I was relieved to find that here I had a highly significant (P=0.01) relationship:

$$S_s = R (a + b \psi) \ldots \ldots A (1)$$

where S_s is what I now called the standard swing, R the rate for the material, and ψ the psi count for the time at which the observation was made (a and b are constants). Thus, since ψ was now known, it was possible to calculate from this formula the standard swing for any material with a rate of R.

My next task was to see if this worked with material in which the charge was induced rather than inherent. For this I selected six specimens: two gravestones with a male rate, as described in Chapter One, one strong and one weak; two with female rates; a flint arrowhead with a strong male rate; and an old pottery shard with a strong female reaction. The radius of gyration of each of these specimens was measured six times, at well-spaced intervals, with the time of day and phase of the moon carefully noted, so that a psi value could be assigned for each measurement. The full results were then subjected to an Analysis of Variance, giving a standard error of ± 2.056 about the overall mean of 106 for the six measurements I had made. During later work I generally took three measurements of each specimen, two in the morning and one in the afternoon, so that the psi counts would be well spread out. Taking a mean of the three measured values obtained, I could generally rely on an error of about ± 3.18 per cent. This would not always be the case however; the method of measuring the radius of gyration described above was to the nearest half centimetre on the scale of the gyrometer. A quarter of a centimetre when the radius was no more than 2 or 3cm was obviously more important than an error of the same size when the radius was over 20cm.

Errors are usually distributed round a mean in what is known as the normal curve, which is bell-shaped, with the peak at the mean value. A distribution of error, where it is largest at low values of the mean and decreases with higher values, is known as a Poisson Distribution, so named after the mathematician who first described it. He was able to show that an error of this type is proportional to the square-root of the mean. With experience I found that I was dealing with values of charge varying from about 20 up to 160. Since the determined error, as found from the Analysis of Variance, was ± 2.056 for a mean of six counts, we can calculate that for a mean of three counts of 20, the error would be ± 6.698 and, for one of 160, would be a ± 2.367. This means that in dealing with comparisons between two means near the lower values of charge, one would have to be very circumspect. However, most observations were with values around 100 and, with a standard error of roughly ± 2.9, I could be fairly certain that two means, separated by as little as 9, were in fact different, with a probability of 1 in 20.

The charge in the specimen, be it male, female or some other rate, I decided to express as a ratio, i.e. the observed radius of gyration (S_o) divided by the calculated standard swing (S_s). Since this can be calculated from equation A(1) shown above, S_s can be substituted by $R(a + b\psi)$. So as to obtain values of a more reasonable size, I decided to multiply this ratio by 100. The charge (C) can therefore be calculated from the equation:

$$C = 100S_o \div R(a + b\psi) \ldots \ldots A(2)$$

This was in fact the state of understanding I had reached when I published the first edition of this book, and I did not give values for the two constants (a and b) in this equation because at that time I believed their values were due to my personal field as reflected in the values of ψ. As has been shown in Chapter 3, my guess that it was I who was varying was wrong. If the stone being measured was screened, it would appear that the varying factor was unnecessary. To check this I carried out two trials using some sixteen materials whose rates covered the whole range. Eight of them were organic and eight inorganic. The gyrometer was surrounded by wire-netting (although I was outside) and the radius of gyration for each was measured first at full moon and then again at the time of the first quarter. The results are plotted in Figure 21, where it will be seen that there is no significant difference between the two sets of figures. It was clear that if the stone is screened, one could obtain a figure for the charge at all times from the equation:

$$C = 100\ S_o \div 0.153\ R \ldots \ldots A(3)$$

(This is using a pendulum bob of 40g and measuring the cord from about 0.5cm below the centre of gravity.)

Following the tradition of the physical sciences, I had to give this unit of charge some suitable name. Although many of the properties I had found in these investigations were in some ways similar to those of electricity, there were many differences, and I was anxious that no false conclusions should be drawn by using similar terms.

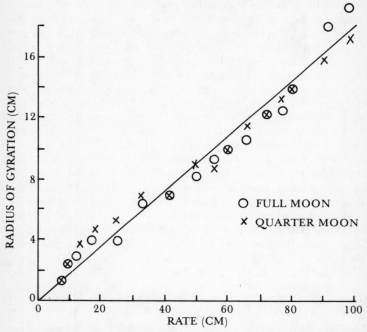

Figure 21. Relationship between radius of gyration and the rate of screened specimens at full and quarter moon.

Since I had called the lines which I had found running through my church 'petrostats', I decided to call this unit of charge a petron and define the standard swing as 100 petrons. Thus, for example, if the observed swing was one-and-a-half times the size of the standard swing for that particular rate, the charge on that specimen would work out at 150 petrons.

2. Using the Psionic Scale

This technique depends on the principle of comparing the charge in the specimen being examined, with the inherent charge of a 'witness', i.e. some substance having the same rate as the specimen. The equipment used is shown in Plate II. It consists of a tape-measure one metre long (B), obtainable at any haberdashery store, at the zero end of which there is a wire loop, used to peg it down using a plastic golf tee (D). The other end of the tape is fixed to a plastic clothes peg, which is used to hold the witness. For the witness I use a piece of sheet zinc (E) for the 60 rate and my gold signet ring for the 72.5 female rate; a small crust of bread in a polythene envelope (F) is used for the 50 rate. I have not as yet discovered any satisfactory witness for the 100 rate; Lethbridge gives for this rate: air, breath, cold, death, deceit, evil and sleep, none of which can be conveniently put in a polythene bag and carried around! However, since this rate is transferable, where it is desired to measure it, I have hammered an untouched stone alongside and brought it back to be measured on the gyrometer. The pendulum used (C) is a short one on about seven inches of chain. Below the bob is a short continuation of chain, used to give an accurate indication of the point at which it swings across the scale. With a pencil and note-pad (G) to record the reading, it all fits neatly into a 12 x 4cm leather purse (H) and can easily be carried in the pocket.

In practice, the zero end of the tape is pinned down with the golf tee close to the specimen being measured, and the appropriate witness clipped into the clothes peg, stretching the tape out away from the specimen. The pendulum is then held somewhere over the middle of the tape and its movements carefully watched. Some dowsers find that it swings diagonally on either side of the correct reading, at which point it should swing straight across the tape. Personally I find that if I have the scale in front of me with the witness and the 100 end to the left and the specimen on the right, the pendulum will gyrate anticlockwise if the reading is too high and clockwise if too low, swinging across the scale at the correct point.

To obtain the value of the charge on the specimen, one compares the length of the scale on either side of this reading, thus:

$$C = 100 \left(\frac{R}{100 - R} \right) \qquad \ldots \ldots \ldots \text{A(4)}$$

where C is the charge in petrons, and R the reading on the scale on the tape measure.

It is possible to make a scale giving a direct reading of the charge, and this is shown on Plate II as A. The charge of 100 is at the 50cm mark and that of 200 at 66.6cm. This explains why the accuracy is so much greater at the lower charges than it is when they are greater than 100 petrons.

As described in Chapter 9, this technique was used to measure the strength of the magnetic field at each ley centre when surveying the Shieldaig peninsula. If it really *was* a magnetic field which I was measuring with a crust of bread as a witness, it should surely be possible to measure that of an actual magnet and express the results in standard units such as Gauss? (See Glossary.) I tried this out with several different magnets and such stones as I believed had a residual magnetic charge (such as Bluestone). Unfortunately I found that there were two difficulties in relating my results measured in petrons to the standard Gauss. Firstly, I had no magnet available of which I was certain of its power in Gauss, but by using the suspected values, I obtained a mean figure of 40 petrons as the equivalent of 1 Gauss; thus a standard swing of 100 petrons for an inherent rate would be equal to 2.5 Gauss. I would not maintain that this figure is exactly correct, but at least it produces results which are within the bounds of reason. Thus the Bluestone had a figure of 1.9 Gauss, dolerite 1.6, and the Rhu-na-Bidh Stone 4.5 Gauss.

The second difficulty was that in all these measurements I made, I had placed the scale either (magnetic) north/south or also east/west. I then found that the east/west figure was always about 18 per cent larger than that obtained when the scale was placed north/south. I thought that this might be due to the influence of the earth's magnetic field, but reversing the scale to point south/north had no effect on the results. Also, one would expect the effect to be constant whatever the power of the magnet (the earth's field is about 0.15 to 0.18 Gauss), whereas this additional charge seems to depend on the size of the charge of the specimen; one of these, an old loud-speaker permanent magnet which I had used in the plant growth experiments described in Chapter Six was very large (several hundred Gauss). In view of this I used only the east/west figures in my field survey work.

Appendix B

1. Charge on two or more stones placed together

The equation to find the charge on two stones at zero separation can be written as follows:

$$C_o = \frac{(C_1 \times M_1) + (C_2 \times M_2)}{M_1 + M_2} \quad \ldots \ldots \ldots A(5)$$

where C_o is the joint charge on the pair of stones at zero separation, C_1 and C_2 are the charges on the two stones with which we are working and which have been previously measured. M_1 and M_2 are their masses (weights) expressed in kilogrammes.

When there are more than two stones, such as in a cairn, this equation can be written as:

$$C_o = \frac{(C_1 \times M_1) + (C_2 \times M_2) + \ldots \ldots (C_n \times M_n)}{M_1 + M_2 + \ldots \ldots M_n} \quad \ldots \ldots A(6)$$

where n is the total number of stones in the pile. This means that the charge on a cairn is made up of the sum of their individual powers divided by the total mass. Thus to measure the overall power of a cairn, if one can estimate the total mass, one has only to multiply this by the overall charge, obtained by hammering a small stone alongside and measuring this with the gyrometer.

2. Loss in strength of a line on separating two charged stones

As explained in Chapter Five, I collected together nine stones of varying weight and charge and arranged them in various combinations of two so that I had twelve pairs with joint powers varying from 0.73 lithons with the smallest ones to 10.75 with the greatest. Each pair was dealt with as previously described (page 82) so that I then had twelve lines similar to those shown in Figure II. Since each pair of stones had a different joint charge at zero separation, I expressed the rate of decrease of strength of the line as a percentage of the full

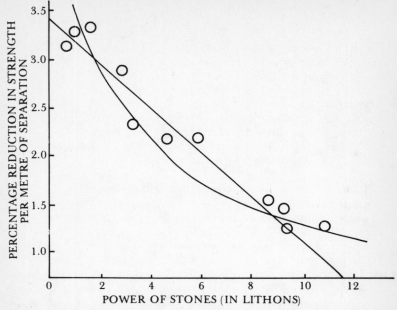

Figure 22. Effect of increasing stone power on percentage reduction in strength of line per metre of separation.

charge. The results of these calculations were plotted against the power of each pair of stones (see Figure 22). Twelve rather scattered points are not very many to draw any firm conclusion from, but it must be realized that to produce these twelve points a great deal of work was entailed. Thus there were twelve pairs of stones, each at six stations, and each measurement was repeated three times, thus making 216 measurements with the gyrometer, together with the labour of moving the stones from one station to another between each measurement. It remained to be seen if I had done enough to get at least some idea of the correct answer.

What I really wanted was some kind of formula by which, given the weight and charge (and hence the power) of two standing stones and the distance separating them, I would be able to calculate the strength of the line between them. Unfortunately, as explained in the text, such a concept is quite impractical, because such stones are not isolated from the environment as my experimental stones in the church had been.

It is quite clear from Figure 22 that the greater the joint power of each pair of stones, the less was the percentage loss in strength in the line as the stones were separated. The question is, whether this is either a direct relationship or something else. To test this I calculated an Analysis of Covariance for the equation:

$$y = a - bx \ldots \ldots A(7)$$

where y is the percentage loss of strength per metre of separation and x the joint power of the two stones. The results of this analysis are plotted as the straight line on the graph.

Let us examine the implications of this straight line. It would seem to indicate that when the joint power of the two stones is zero there would be a percentage loss in strength per metre of 3.4 and that at a percentage loss of zero the joint power would be only 15.9 lithons. On the face of it, both these predictions seem pretty unlikely. I therefore tried altering the equation to:

$$y = \frac{1}{c + dx} \ldots \ldots A(8)$$

and tried another Analysis of Covariance, which then gave me the curved line shown in Figure 22. This suggests that at zero power the loss per metre is infinite, while at a power of 1 lithon the loss would be 3.35 per cent. At a 1000 lithons the predicted loss is only 0.00577 per cent per metre and it never falls to zero however large the power. This, therefore, seems to be the more reasonable solution. These analyses also showed that the second equation, giving the curved line, was a slightly better fit to the points and that the relationship was in fact highly significant (P=0.01). From this I was then able to produce the required formula:

$$S_L = C_o - \left(\frac{C_o \times D}{24.4 + 5.45 \, \Sigma \, P} \right) \ldots \ldots A(9)$$

In this, S is the strength of the line between the two stones, which is what we are trying to determine. The stones have a combined power of Σ P expressed in lithons, and are separated by a distance of D metres. We first have to calculate the combined charge of the two stones when at zero separation (C_o) by using equation A (5) and from this subtracting the factor within the brackets. It will be seen that this factor is increased as distance D increases, but decreases as Σ P grows larger. The two constants (24.4 and 5.45) are derived from the analysis of the curved line in Figure 22.

This equation is called A(9) throughout the text and was subsequently used to calculate the strength of the line between two stones when their weight and charge were known, together with the distance separating them. It must be made clear that this equation only holds good for two stones in isolation from all other influences. As shown in the text, if there are other charged stones in the vicinity, a far more complex situation arises, which is not covered by this equation.

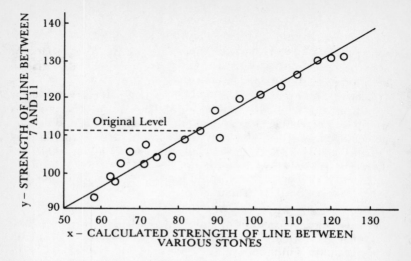

Figure 23. Strength of line between stones 7 and 11, with external
line of various strengths.

3. Strength of a Three Stone Line

Since two stones do not make up a classic ley line, I had to see what
would happen if I added a third stone to the pairs I had already
studied. To examine this, two stones (Nos 7 and 11) were set up on
the church gallery 13 feet apart, giving a line between them with a
strength of 112.3 petrons. Five other stones with powers ranging
from 0.336 to 5.915 lithons were then placed in turn at distances of
10, 20, 30 and 40 feet from stone No 7. In each case the strength of
the line between stones 7 and 11 was measured with the gyrometer
(see Figure 23).

From equation A(9) (above) it was possible to calculate the theoretical strength of the line between stone 7 and the various added
stones, ignoring stone 11 on the other side. I had also measured the
strength of the line between 7 and 11 in each case, so I had a set of
twenty pairs of figures. These results were subjected to an Analysis of
Covariance, giving a 'highly significant' relation:

$$y = 63.4 + 0.563 \ x \qquad \ldots \ldots \ . \ A \ (10)$$

where 'y' is the strength of the line between stones 7 and 11, and 'x'
the calculated strength of the line beyond stone 7 (i.e. between it and
and the various other stones).

Now, I noted that the mean value of 'y' was 112.3, which is very
near the value of the strength of the line between stones 7 and 11

(111.3) before the extra stones were added beyond stone 7. I also noted that y varied from 93.0 to 131.7 (see Figure 23). The mean of the calculated values of the line beyond stone 7 was 86.8, varying from 53.0 to 123.9. This meant that raising the external line above the figure of 86.9 had increased the strength of the line between stones 7 and 11, and that decreasing the external line below this value had decreased the strength of the line between 7 and 11 below the figure at which it had been before any external stones were added. This obviously complicated the situation considerably. It was no good my going out and measuring the size and charge of two standing stones, together with the distance between them, and then hoping to calculate the strength of the intervening line with the aid of equation A(9). These stones would inevitably have lines extending from them, in both directions, to other stones in the ley line, and these would influence the line under consideration. In fact, further investigation showed that the situation was still more complicated than it had so far proved to be.

It will be remembered that the strength of the line beyond stone 7 had been calculated, when various stones had been placed in line and varied in distance, by means of equation A(9). I thought it would be a good idea to check these external lines: if the line between 7 and 11 could be altered by varying the external line, that external line could surely be altered by reversing this procedure, even though the distance between 7 and 11 was fixed throughout the experiment. I therefore reversed the whole process of the previous experiment

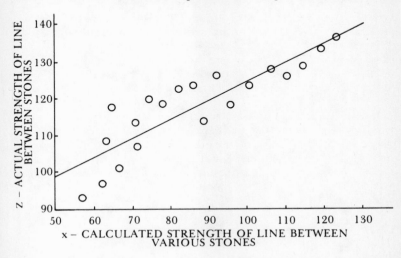

Figure 24. Relation betwen calculated and measured strength of external line.

and this time measured the strength of the lines between stone 7 and those set out at varying distances. On plotting this gave a good straight line (Figure 24), which on analysis produced the equation:

$$Z = 75.28 + 0.4887 \, x \ldots \ldots \, A(11)$$

where x is the calculated strength of these lines, as in equation A(9), and Z is the actual value as measured with the gyrometer. This means that by adding the line between stones 7 and 11, which originally had a value of 111.3, the strength of the lines between stone 7 and the various stones used had been increased above their calculated values, although this increase was inversely proportional to the size of the original value.

Appendix C

Masking a stone with quartz chips

I wanted to know the quantity of quartz chips required to mask a charged stone of given weight and whether this varied with the weight of that stone. I decided that the best way to determine this was to set up two stones on the church gallery, screened at both ends so that if one stone was completely masked, there would be no line between them. Various quartz chips weighing from 0.26 to 10.75 g were placed on one of the stones, the weight of which was known, and the strength of the line between the stones measured with the gyrometer. This procedure was then repeated with six other stones of different weight. (Unfortunately it was not possible to detect the point of complete masking, because the reaction of the pendulum would become too small as this point was approached). The strengths of the line were plotted against the weight of chips used and, as this proved to be a linear relationship, the line could be extrapolated back to determine the weight of chips needed to give complete masking for each of the seven stones.

As I have said, I wanted to know the weight of chips required to give complete masking of a stone of given weight. I therefore divided the weight of chips required for each stone by the weight of that stone in kilogrammes, thus obtaining the weight of chips required per kilogramme of stone. These figures were then plotted against the weight of each stone (Figure 25, curve 0). It appeared from this that the relationship was inverse, so I then replotted the graph, this time using the reciprocal of the figures for the weights of the chips. This gave a good straight line (line X). Analysis of Covariance of these figures gave the best straight line which could be drawn through these seven points and a coefficient r=0.9766.

I was still not satisfied that the best figures had been obtained from this investigation. I therefore plotted the reciprocal of the weight of the chips against the *power* of the stones instead of their weight. This seemed at the time to be a more reasonable hypothesis, since it was the power of the stones to form a line which one was

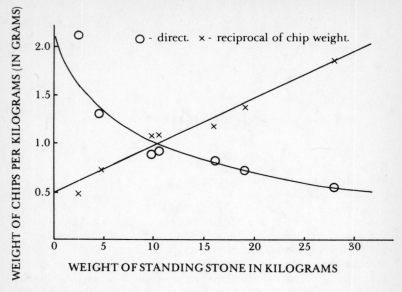

Figure 25. Weight of quartz chips per kilo of stone required to mask
power of standing stone.

trying to mask and one might have thought that the size of the
charge, as well as the weight of the stone, might be important.
However, on analysis of these figures, I obtained a coefficient of
r=0.9206, which is probably not significantly worse than that for the
weights, but is tending in that direction. I therefore concluded that
the weight of quartz chips is more probably related to the weight of
the stone concerned. From the analysis I obtained the equation:

$$\frac{1}{y} = 0.5045 + 0.04763x \quad \ldots \ldots \ldots A\,(12)$$

where y is the weight (in grammes) of quartz chips per kilogramme
of stone required to completely mask a stone weighing 'x' kg.

Glossary

Aquastat This is one of the three types of *geodetic line* described by Underwood, and on which he claimed ancient buildings were sited. Aquastats appear to differ from the straight lines found by the present writer in buildings and here termed *Petrostats* in that they consist of only two sets of triads with no central line and usually do not run straight. In spite of their name, aquastats do not appear to be associated with water.

Black Lines Defined[25] as a *dowsable energy line* which is identified by the use of the colour black as a *witness* and associated with the transfer to a site of influences adverse to mental or physical health.

Black Stream A term used by water diviners to denote an underground stream that reacts to a black on the *Mager Circle* and which is not considered drinkable. Some dowsers think that such 'streams' give off rays which are harmful to the health of anyone living within their range.

Blind Springs Described by Underwood as forming the centre of a primary spiral to which primary *geodetic lines* converge. Many dowsers have confirmed that *ley centres* are sited over blind springs. It is not certain that these blind springs are necessarily connected with underground water.

Bluestone An igneous rock used at Stonehenge and known as 'prescellite'. It occurs only at the eastern end of the Prescelly Range in South Wales. It is also known as 'spotted dolerite' since it contains nodules of quarz.

Charge   This is the property of material which causes the pendulum of a dowser to gyrate. A charge may be inherent or induced, and its magnitude is measured with a gyrometer in terms of *petrons*.

Circadian   A term introduced by Franz Halberg et al. (in *Photoperiodism and Related Phenomena in Plants and Animals*, Washington, 1959) to denote a rhythm with a natural period of about twenty-four hours. A circalunar rhythm has a natural period of about 29.5 solar days.

Crossing Stone   A term used by the present writer to designate a stone that marks the spot where two or more energy lines cross. A crossing stone differs from a *ley centre* in that it is not situated over a *blind spring* or geomagnetic field.

Decay Rate   The process in which the charge is lost from an object such as a stone, when it has been moved from a charged field. It is shown that the decay rate is constant whatever the charge and that it is exponential in form with a half-life of about three hours.

Dowsable Energy Line   Defined as an energy line whose presence and direction can be determined by dowsing. [25] Such lines can be above or below ground and it is probable that all *ley lines* are Dowsable Energy Lines.

Field   The area surrounding a charged object in which the *pendulum* reacts to the charge. T.C. Lethbridge noted that this field was in the form of a circle of a radius equal to the *rate* of the field. This circle, he stated, formed the base of cones extending both above and below the object.

Fixing   A process described by the writer, by which the *charge* is permanently fixed into an object placed within the field of another charged object. Without this process of fixing, the charge taken up by the object gradually decreases (decays) when removed from the field, and is ultimately lost.

Gauss One of a number of units used to measure the flux density of a magnet. Defined as the flux which will induce an electromotive force of one abvolt per centimetre in a wire moving across the field at a velocity of one centimetre per second.

Geodetic Line Strictly, the shortest line between two points on a curved surface. This term was used rather loosely by Underwood to denote any *dowsable energy line* which could be detected below the earth's surface, although most of these are certainly not the shortest path.

Geomancer One who practises the art of divination by means of signs derived from the Earth. An art practised in ancient China [12] and possibly the equivalent of the more modern term 'environmentalist'.

Gyrometer An instrument designed by the author for measuring the radius of gyration of a pendulum held by a dowser over a charged object. This records what is termed the *observed swing* at the time.

Induced Charge When an object, for example a stone, is placed within the field of another charged object, it takes up that charge, which is then said to be induced. This will ultimately decay away when the object is removed from the field unless it is *fixed*. The induced charge is measured in *'petrons'*.

Inherent Charge T.C. Lethbridge showed that all objects, and even abstract ideas such as courage, country of origin etc., have an inherent charge which is related to the length of the pendulum cord (*rate*) used to detect it. The present writer has been able to show that if the *'radius of gyration'* of an inherent charge, i.e. the *'standard swing'*, is divided by the appropriate rate, a constant is obtained.

Intermediate Line An energy line, similar to a *ley line* in all aspects except that it flows only between two adjoining *ley centres* and therefore does not constitute an alignment.

Interrupters A term introduced by Lethbridge to denote

the property of certain materials which, when placed within the *field* of another substance, interrupt the appropriate gyrations of the pendulum. He noted that they can have a variety of properties, having their own *rate*, and perhaps a *vital rate*, but interrupt that of another. An interrupter may reverse the vital rate or neutralize another interrupter. There are many variations of this property.

Ley Centre   Here defined as a charged point that lies over a *blind spring* and *crossed streams*, and from which radiate *ley lines* — usually seven in number. The pendulum always reacts at such a centre to the rate of 50, thus indicating the presence of a geomagnetic field.

Ley Lines   Defined by Devereux and Thomson [11] as alignments of sites which ley hunters believe were surveyed and marked in pre-history, the generally accepted criterion being five such sites in 25 miles. Many dowsers believe that only such alignments as are also *dowsable energy lines* should be considered to be genuine ley lines.

Lithon   (from the Greek *lithos,* meaning a stone). A unit of power of a charged stone etc. It is the product of the *charge* (measured in *petrons*), multiplied by the mass (in terms of kilogrammes). Thus a stone weighing 1kg with a charge of 100 petrons is said to have a power of 1 lithon.

Long Pendulum   The type of dowsing pendulum described by Lethbridge. It has a cord 40 inches long and each concept has its own length of cord, called the *rate* at which the pendulum will gyrate. The present writer uses a pendulum with a cord 1m in length and the rates are measured in centimetres from the centre of gravity of the plumb bob to the point at which the cord is held. The cord is marked every 10cm with a coloured bead to facilitate measurement.

Mager Circle   A disc divided into eight coloured segments, commonly used as a *witness* by water diviners to test the potability of underground water. The disc is usually held in one hand at the appropriate colour while using the pendulum. The colours of the segments, going clockwise, are: black, white, purple, green, yellow, red, and grey. The actual colour assigned to a property varies somewhat between dowsers. Other things besides water can also give a reaction to a Mager colour: thus a 'positive' (male) energy line gives a reaction with the pendulum to the colour blue, and a 'negative' (female) line to white. Each colour also has its own Lethbridge *rate*.

Masking   A term used in this work to denote the effect of an *interrupter* on a charged stone. It does not remove the charge, but if present in sufficient quantity the interrupter effectively prevents the charge having any external influence. On removing the interrupter, the charge reappears, proving that it had only been masked.

Megalithic   (from the Greek for large stone). A term commonly used for any structure built of large stones, usually set upright in the earth and dating, in Western Europe, from 5000 to 500 BC. In this book the term megalithic man is used simply to denote the builders of these monuments, whoever they may have been. It is clear that over such an extended period of time their cultural and racial characteristics must have changed considerably.

Observed Swing   The *radius of gyration* of the pendulum when held over a charged specimen. This radius is measured by means of a *gyrometer*. It varies according to the *rate*, the *charge* of the specimen, and, if not screened, also with the time of the observation.

Overground   A term proposed by Tom Graves [21] to denote any *dowsable energy line* which flows above ground, as compared with Underwood's *geodetic lines* which flow below ground.

Parallel   A term used by Underwood to describe the parallel lines which run on either side of a central *geodetic line*, at a distance equal to the *rate*. They appear to be made up of the outer edge of the line of circular fields surrounding the central line. There is some evidence that there is a further pair of parallels at a distance of 5½ times that of the inner ones.

Petron   (from the Greek *petros*, a rock). A unit of *charge* of a stone or other object. It is defined as the ratio between the *standard swing* for a particular *rate* and the *observed swing* of the pendulum, the former being taken as 100. Thus, if the standard swing is calculated as being a *radius of gyration* of 10cm, and the observed swing is found to be 15cm, the specimen in question is said to have a charge of 150 petrons.

Petrostat   A term used by the writer to designate a straight, charged, dowsable line running through a stone building. In view of the fact that it seems to have the same properties as a *ley line*, it can probably be considered as equivalent, although it obviously does not fit the generally accepted definition of a ley alignment.

Polarity   Many dowsers maintain that *charge*, *power* and *strength* can be either positive (rate 60) or negative (rate 72.5). These are said to be equivalent to male/female and to Yang/Yin. Lines also appear to indicate a colour on the *Mager Circle* the male/positive lines being blue, and the female/negative lines being white. This is said to relate to the Blue Dragon and White Tiger in ancient Chinese Geomancy, as described by Eitel. [12]

Power   The property of a charged stone that enables it to radiate energy lines. The power is defined as the product of the *charge* multiplied by the mass (weight). The degree of power is measured in *lithons*.

Psi Factor   (from the Greek letter ψ, psi). A term introduced by Lethbridge as a measure of the psychic potential of a dowser. It is measured by the number of gyrations of the pendulum with a cord 22.5cm long before it starts to oscillate. The present writer found that the value of the psi factor varies with the phases of the moon and also has a *circadian* rhythm.

Psionic Scale   A method of measuring the strength of a *charge* on an object by comparing it with another object of known value, described as the *witness*. This method was outlined by Reyner [39] and is fully described in Appendix A(2).

Radius of Gyration   The radius of a circle round which a pendulum gyrates when it is held by a dowser over a charged specimen. The radius varies in size with the *rate* and also the *psi factor*, if not screened. It is measured in centimetres with a *gyrometer*.

Rate   A term introduced by Lethbridge to indicate the length of the cord of a dowser's pendulum. Everything has its own specific rate, although, of course, some rates are common to several different objects or concepts. In this book the rate is measured in centimetres from the centre of gravity of the bob to the point on the cord at which it is held by the dowser.

Remanence   When an object having dowsable energy is moved from a site, it usually leaves some signs of that energy which can still be detected by dowsing. These signs gradually decay away over a longer or shorter period unless they have been *fixed*. Remanence can also occur with a magnetic field.

Short Pendulum   This is the pendulum used by the majority of dowsers. It usually has a cord about 15-20cm long, and is used to reply to a specific mental question posed by the dowser, either by oscillating, or by gyrating in a clockwise or anticlockwise direction. The interpretation of the response varies with the individual dowser. The form of the question has to be chosen with great care or an ambiguous reply may be returned.

SPIN   A Segmented, Polycentric, Integrated Network. A term first used in the Social Sciences and here used to describe the close integration of a complex of *ley centres*.

Standard Swing   The *radius of gyration* of the pendulum when measuring the *inherent charge* of the specimen. For a given *rate*, the standard swing can be calculated from the equation given in Appendix A(1).

Strength   A measure of the dowsable energy in a line, be it a *ley line*, a *petrostat*, an *aquastat*, etc. For any given appropriate *rate*, the strength can be measured by observing the *radius of gyration* with a *gyrometer*, and can thus be defined in terms of *petrons*.

Triad   A term introduced by Underwood to describe the form of many *geodetic lines*. Thus, each main line is made up of three minor lines, which together form a triad.

Vital Rates   This term is here used for the two *rates* of 60 and 72.5, rather than calling them the two 'sex' rates, since this could cause confusion with the true rate for sex which is 40. All living material possesses a rate for either male (60) or female (72.5), and these rates have the unusual property of being transferable to non-living material such as stone.

Water Line   A particular type of *geodetic line* described by Underwood and thought by him to indicate a flow of underground water. Except that water lines do not run in straight lines or above ground, they seem to have similar dowsing characteristics to *ley lines*, i.e. a central triad with *parallel* triads at some distance on either side.

Witness   Usually defined as a sample of the material being sought by the dowser and used to make his dowsing more sensitive; it is generally held in the hand with the pendulum etc. This term is here used to describe a sample of material having the same *rate* as the object being measured with the *Psionic Scale* and with which it is compared.

References

1 Atkinson, R.J.C., *Stonehenge*, 2nd Ed. Harmondsworth (1979).

2 Backster, Cleve., 'Evidence of a Primary Perception in Plant Life', *International Journal of Parapsychology* (Winter 1986).

3 Beadon, C.V., 'Ley Lines and Black Streams — Fact or Fancies?', *Journal of the British Society of Dowsers*, XXVII, 242 (1980).

4 Bohm, David, *Wholeness and the Implicate Order*, Routledge and Kegan Paul (1980).

5 Bolton, B.L., *The Secret Power of Plants*, Abacus (1975).

6 Bose, J.C., *Response in the Living and Non-Living*, Longman, Green and Co. (1922).

7 Brennan, Martin, *The Boyne Valley Vision,* Dolman Press, (1980).

8 Burgess, Colin, *The Age of Stonehenge*, Dent (1984).

9 Burl, Aubrey, *Circles of Stone*, Weidenfeld and Nicholson (1979).

10 Burr, H.S. *Blueprint for Immortality*, Neville Spearman (1971).

11 Devereux, P. and Thomson, Ian, *The Ley Hunter's Companion,* Thames and Hudson (1979).

[12] Eitel, E.J., *Feng Shui*, Pentacle Books (1979).

[13] Fenwick, N., 'Leys and Ley Lines: What are they are they all talking about?', *Practical Geomancy*, 1,2, 4-8 (1986).

[14] Fidler, J.H. 'Dating with the Pendulum', *Journal of the British Society of Dowsers,* XXIV, 45 (1974).

[15] Fidler, J.H., 'With a Pendulum amongst the Larachs', *Journal of the British Society of Dowsers,* XXV, 178 (1976).

[16] Fidler, J.H. 'Mulitdimensional Leys', *The Ley Hunter*, 83 (1978).

[17] Fidler, J.H., 'A Technique for the Measurement of the Energy of Ley Lines by Dowsing', *Journal of the British Society of Dowsers,* XXVII, 175 (1980).

[18] Fidler, J.H., 'Some Aspects of Ley Line Energy', *Journal of the British Society of Dowsers*, 31, 1 (1985).

[19] Fidler, J.H., 'Earth Energy Lines and Eclipses', *Journal of the British Society of Dowsers*, 32, 36 (1987).

[20] Grad, Bernard, 'A Telekinetic Effect on Plant Growth', *International Journal of Parapsychology,* V, 2 (1963) and VI, 4 (1964).

[21] Graves, Tom, *Needles of Stone*, Turnstone Books, (1978).

[22] Guest, M., 'A Survey of Deraying Techniques', *Journal of the British Society of Dowsers,* 31, 111-122 (1985).

[23] Jenkins, Stephen, *Undiscovered Country*, Neville Spearman (1977).

[24] Jones, A.V. 'Accident or Design?', *Journal of the British Society of Dowsers,* XXVIII, 194 (1981).

[25] Laver, F.J.M. 'Contributions to Clarification of Dowsing Terminology', *Journal of the British Society of Dowsers,* 31, 213-226 (1986).

[26] Lee, E.W., *Magnetism*, Penguin Books (1963).

[27] Lethbridge, T.C.:
 [a] *ESP, Beyond Time and Distance*, RKP (1965).
 [b] *A Step in the Dark*, RKP (1967).
 [c] *The Monkey's Tail*, RKP (1969).
 [d] *The Legend of the Sons of God,* RKP (1972).
 [e] *The Power of the Pendulum,* RKP (1976).

[28] Loehr, Revd Franklin, *The Power of Prayer on Plants*, New American Library (1969).

[29] Lonegren, Sig, 'Notes from New England', *The Ley Hunter*, 91 (1981).

[30] Lonegren, Sig, 'Pseudo-Geomancy', *The Ley Hunter,* 99, 24 (1985).

[31] Maby, J.C. and Franklin, T.B., *The Physics of the Dowsing Rod*, Bell (1949).

[32] Michell, John, *City of Revelation*, Garnstone Press (1979).

[33] Miller, R.N., 'Methods of Detecting and Measuring Healing Energies', in *Future Science*, Ed. White and Krippner, Anchor Books (1977).

[34] Newham, C.A., 'Stonehenge, a Neolithic Observatory', *Nature*, 211, 456-468 (1966).

[35] Petitpierre, Dom Robert, *Exorcising Devils*, Robert Hale (1976).

[36] Pitts, M.W., 'On the Road to Stonehenge'. *Proc. Prehistoric Society*, 48, 78-132 (1982)

[37] Popper, Karl, *Unended Quest*, Fontana (1982).

[38] Reichenbach, Carl von, *The Mysterious Odic Force,* Aquarian Press (1977).

[39] Reyner, J.H., *Psionic Medicine*, RKP (1977).

40 Robins, Don, *Circles of Silence,* Souvenier Press (1985).

41 Robins, G.V., 'Earth Currents — The Possible Influence of Quartz', *The Ley Hunter*, 75, 3 (1975).

42 Robins, G.V., 'Images in Stone', *The Ley Hunter,* 76, 11, and 77, 14 (1977).

43 Ryecroft, M., 'A View of the upper Atmosphere from Antarctica'. *New Scientist*, 44 (28th November, 1985).

44 Screeton, Paul, *Quicksilver Heritage*, Thorsons (1974).

45 Smith, Sister Dr Justa, 'Significant Results in Enzyme Activity from a Healer's Hands', *Newsletter*, Parapsychology Foundation (Jan–Feb. 1969).

46 Thom, A. and Thom, A.S., *Megalithic Remains in Britain and Brittany,* Oxford, (1980).

47 Thompkins, P. and Bird, C., *The Secret Life of Plants,* Allen Lane (1974).

48 Underwood, Guy, *The Pattern of the Past*, Museum Press (1969).

49 Watkins, Alfred, *The Old Straight Track*, Methuen (1925).

50 Watkins, Alfred, *The Ley Hunter's Manual*, Simpkin Marshall (1927). [Reprinted with introduction by John Michell, Turnstone Press (1983).]

51 Williams, P., 'European Radar Unscrambles the Ionosphere', *New Scientist*, 46 (5th December 1985).

52 Williams, T. and Belamy, L., *Ley Lines in Question,* World Works (1983).

53 Wooster, Sarah, 'New Concepts in Earth Mysteries/Earth Energies', *Journal of the British Society of Dowsers,* 31, 289-299 (1986).

Index